C-587   CAREER EXAMINATION SERIES

This is your
PASSBOOK for...

Pipefitter

Test Preparation Study Guide
Questions & Answers

COPYRIGHT NOTICE

This book is SOLELY intended for, is sold ONLY to, and its use is RESTRICTED to individual, bona fide applicants or candidates who qualify by virtue of having seriously filed applications for appropriate license, certificate, professional and/or promotional advancement, higher school matriculation, scholarship, or other legitimate requirements of education and/or governmental authorities.

This book is NOT intended for use, class instruction, tutoring, training, duplication, copying, reprinting, excerption, or adaptation, etc., by:

1) Other publishers
2) Proprietors and/or Instructors of "Coaching" and/or Preparatory Courses
3) Personnel and/or Training Divisions of commercial, industrial, and governmental organizations
4) Schools, colleges, or universities and/or their departments and staffs, including teachers and other personnel
5) Testing Agencies or Bureaus
6) Study groups which seek by the purchase of a single volume to copy and/or duplicate and/or adapt this material for use by the group as a whole without having purchased individual volumes for each of the members of the group
7) Et al.

Such persons would be in violation of appropriate Federal and State statutes.

PROVISION OF LICENSING AGREEMENTS – Recognized educational, commercial, industrial, and governmental institutions and organizations, and others legitimately engaged in educational pursuits, including training, testing, and measurement activities, may address request for a licensing agreement to the copyright owners, who will determine whether, and under what conditions, including fees and charges, the materials in this book may be used them. In other words, a licensing facility exists for the legitimate use of the material in this book on other than an individual basis. However, it is asseverated and affirmed here that the material in this book CANNOT be used without the receipt of the express permission of such a licensing agreement from the Publishers. Inquiries re licensing should be addressed to the company, attention rights and permissions department.

All rights reserved, including the right of reproduction in whole or in part, in any form or by any means, electronic or mechanical, including photocopying, recording, or by any information storage and retrieval system, without permission in writing from the Publisher.

Copyright © 2024 by
National Learning Corporation

212 Michael Drive, Syosset, NY 11791
(516) 921-8888 • www.passbooks.com
E-mail: info@passbooks.com

PASSBOOK® SERIES

THE *PASSBOOK® SERIES* has been created to prepare applicants and candidates for the ultimate academic battlefield – the examination room.

At some time in our lives, each and every one of us may be required to take an examination – for validation, matriculation, admission, qualification, registration, certification, or licensure.

Based on the assumption that every applicant or candidate has met the basic formal educational standards, has taken the required number of courses, and read the necessary texts, the *PASSBOOK® SERIES* furnishes the one special preparation which may assure passing with confidence, instead of failing with insecurity. Examination questions – together with answers – are furnished as the basic vehicle for study so that the mysteries of the examination and its compounding difficulties may be eliminated or diminished by a sure method.

This book is meant to help you pass your examination provided that you qualify and are serious in your objective.

The entire field is reviewed through the huge store of content information which is succinctly presented through a provocative and challenging approach – the question-and-answer method.

A climate of success is established by furnishing the correct answers at the end of each test.

You soon learn to recognize types of questions, forms of questions, and patterns of questioning. You may even begin to anticipate expected outcomes.

You perceive that many questions are repeated or adapted so that you can gain acute insights, which may enable you to score many sure points.

You learn how to confront new questions, or types of questions, and to attack them confidently and work out the correct answers.

You note objectives and emphases, and recognize pitfalls and dangers, so that you may make positive educational adjustments.

Moreover, you are kept fully informed in relation to new concepts, methods, practices, and directions in the field.

You discover that you are actually taking the examination all the time: you are preparing for the examination by "taking" an examination, not by reading extraneous and/or supererogatory textbooks.

In short, this PASSBOOK®, used directedly, should be an important factor in helping you to pass your test.

PIPEFITTER

DUTIES AND RESPONSIBILITIES
Under direction, lays and fits cast iron bell and spigot water mains; performs related work.

EXAMPLES OF TYPICAL TASKS
Centers and sets pipes, elbows, crosses, valves and plugs. Cuts pipes to required dimensions. Yarns, melts and pours lead, and fits by hand or by pneumatic hammer and tools. Directs the work of assigned helpers. Reads department distribution maps. Keeps records and prepares reports.

SUBJECT OF EXAMINATION
The written test will be of the multiple-choice type and may include questions on:
1. Knowledge of materials, fittings, tools and equipment used in pipefitting work;
2. Knowledge of materials, methods and equipment used in excavation and backfilling;
3. Ability to read and understand instructions, and interpret water distribution maps;
4. Ability to perform basic mathematical computations;
5. Knowledge of pertinent codes and rules and regulations;
6. Knowledge of report writing, record keeping, safety, and supervision of subordinate personnel; and
7. Other related areas.

HOW TO TAKE A TEST

I. YOU MUST PASS AN EXAMINATION

A. WHAT EVERY CANDIDATE SHOULD KNOW

Examination applicants often ask us for help in preparing for the written test. What can I study in advance? What kinds of questions will be asked? How will the test be given? How will the papers be graded?

As an applicant for a civil service examination, you may be wondering about some of these things. Our purpose here is to suggest effective methods of advance study and to describe civil service examinations.

Your chances for success on this examination can be increased if you know how to prepare. Those "pre-examination jitters" can be reduced if you know what to expect. You can even experience an adventure in good citizenship if you know why civil service exams are given.

B. WHY ARE CIVIL SERVICE EXAMINATIONS GIVEN?

Civil service examinations are important to you in two ways. As a citizen, you want public jobs filled by employees who know how to do their work. As a job seeker, you want a fair chance to compete for that job on an equal footing with other candidates. The best-known means of accomplishing this two-fold goal is the competitive examination.

Exams are widely publicized throughout the nation. They may be administered for jobs in federal, state, city, municipal, town or village governments or agencies.

Any citizen may apply, with some limitations, such as the age or residence of applicants. Your experience and education may be reviewed to see whether you meet the requirements for the particular examination. When these requirements exist, they are reasonable and applied consistently to all applicants. Thus, a competitive examination may cause you some uneasiness now, but it is your privilege and safeguard.

C. HOW ARE CIVIL SERVICE EXAMS DEVELOPED?

Examinations are carefully written by trained technicians who are specialists in the field known as "psychological measurement," in consultation with recognized authorities in the field of work that the test will cover. These experts recommend the subject matter areas or skills to be tested; only those knowledges or skills important to your success on the job are included. The most reliable books and source materials available are used as references. Together, the experts and technicians judge the difficulty level of the questions.

Test technicians know how to phrase questions so that the problem is clearly stated. Their ethics do not permit "trick" or "catch" questions. Questions may have been tried out on sample groups, or subjected to statistical analysis, to determine their usefulness.

Written tests are often used in combination with performance tests, ratings of training and experience, and oral interviews. All of these measures combine to form the best-known means of finding the right person for the right job.

II. HOW TO PASS THE WRITTEN TEST

A. NATURE OF THE EXAMINATION

To prepare intelligently for civil service examinations, you should know how they differ from school examinations you have taken. In school you were assigned certain definite pages to read or subjects to cover. The examination questions were quite detailed and usually emphasized memory. Civil service exams, on the other hand, try to discover your present ability to perform the duties of a position, plus your potentiality to learn these duties. In other words, a civil service exam attempts to predict how successful you will be. Questions cover such a broad area that they cannot be as minute and detailed as school exam questions.

In the public service similar kinds of work, or positions, are grouped together in one "class." This process is known as *position-classification*. All the positions in a class are paid according to the salary range for that class. One class title covers all of these positions, and they are all tested by the same examination.

B. FOUR BASIC STEPS

1) Study the announcement

How, then, can you know what subjects to study? Our best answer is: "Learn as much as possible about the class of positions for which you've applied." The exam will test the knowledge, skills and abilities needed to do the work.

Your most valuable source of information about the position you want is the official exam announcement. This announcement lists the training and experience qualifications. Check these standards and apply only if you come reasonably close to meeting them.

The brief description of the position in the examination announcement offers some clues to the subjects which will be tested. Think about the job itself. Review the duties in your mind. Can you perform them, or are there some in which you are rusty? Fill in the blank spots in your preparation.

Many jurisdictions preview the written test in the exam announcement by including a section called "Knowledge and Abilities Required," "Scope of the Examination," or some similar heading. Here you will find out specifically what fields will be tested.

2) Review your own background

Once you learn in general what the position is all about, and what you need to know to do the work, ask yourself which subjects you already know fairly well and which need improvement. You may wonder whether to concentrate on improving your strong areas or on building some background in your fields of weakness. When the announcement has specified "some knowledge" or "considerable knowledge," or has used adjectives like "beginning principles of..." or "advanced ... methods," you can get a clue as to the number and difficulty of questions to be asked in any given field. More questions, and hence broader coverage, would be included for those subjects which are more important in the work. Now weigh your strengths and weaknesses against the job requirements and prepare accordingly.

3) Determine the level of the position

Another way to tell how intensively you should prepare is to understand the level of the job for which you are applying. Is it the entering level? In other words, is this the position in which beginners in a field of work are hired? Or is it an intermediate or advanced level? Sometimes this is indicated by such words as "Junior" or "Senior" in the class title. Other jurisdictions use Roman numerals to designate the level – Clerk I, Clerk II, for example. The word "Supervisor" sometimes appears in the title. If the level is not indicated by the title, check the description of duties. Will you be working under very close supervision, or will you have responsibility for independent decisions in this work?

4) Choose appropriate study materials

Now that you know the subjects to be examined and the relative amount of each subject to be covered, you can choose suitable study materials. For beginning level jobs, or even advanced ones, if you have a pronounced weakness in some aspect of your training, read a modern, standard textbook in that field. Be sure it is up to date and has general coverage. Such books are normally available at your library, and the librarian will be glad to help you locate one. For entry-level positions, questions of appropriate difficulty are chosen -- neither highly advanced questions, nor those too simple. Such questions require careful thought but not advanced training.

If the position for which you are applying is technical or advanced, you will read more advanced, specialized material. If you are already familiar with the basic principles of your field, elementary textbooks would waste your time. Concentrate on advanced textbooks and technical periodicals. Think through the concepts and review difficult problems in your field.

These are all general sources. You can get more ideas on your own initiative, following these leads. For example, training manuals and publications of the government agency which employs workers in your field can be useful, particularly for technical and professional positions. A letter or visit to the government department involved may result in more specific study suggestions, and certainly will provide you with a more definite idea of the exact nature of the position you are seeking.

III. KINDS OF TESTS

Tests are used for purposes other than measuring knowledge and ability to perform specified duties. For some positions, it is equally important to test ability to make adjustments to new situations or to profit from training. In others, basic mental abilities not dependent on information are essential. Questions which test these things may not appear as pertinent to the duties of the position as those which test for knowledge and information. Yet they are often highly important parts of a fair examination. For very general questions, it is almost impossible to help you direct your study efforts. What we can do is to point out some of the more common of these general abilities needed in public service positions and describe some typical questions.

1) General information

Broad, general information has been found useful for predicting job success in some kinds of work. This is tested in a variety of ways, from vocabulary lists to questions about current events. Basic background in some field of work, such as sociology or economics, may be sampled in a group of questions. Often these are principles which have become familiar to most persons through exposure rather than through formal training. It is difficult to advise you how to study for these questions; being alert to the world around you is our best suggestion.

2) Verbal ability

An example of an ability needed in many positions is verbal or language ability. Verbal ability is, in brief, the ability to use and understand words. Vocabulary and grammar tests are typical measures of this ability. Reading comprehension or paragraph interpretation questions are common in many kinds of civil service tests. You are given a paragraph of written material and asked to find its central meaning.

3) Numerical ability

Number skills can be tested by the familiar arithmetic problem, by checking paired lists of numbers to see which are alike and which are different, or by interpreting charts and graphs. In the latter test, a graph may be printed in the test booklet which you are asked to use as the basis for answering questions.

4) Observation

A popular test for law-enforcement positions is the observation test. A picture is shown to you for several minutes, then taken away. Questions about the picture test your ability to observe both details and larger elements.

5) Following directions

In many positions in the public service, the employee must be able to carry out written instructions dependably and accurately. You may be given a chart with several columns, each column listing a variety of information. The questions require you to carry out directions involving the information given in the chart.

6) Skills and aptitudes

Performance tests effectively measure some manual skills and aptitudes. When the skill is one in which you are trained, such as typing or shorthand, you can practice. These tests are often very much like those given in business school or high school courses. For many of the other skills and aptitudes, however, no short-time preparation can be made. Skills and abilities natural to you or that you have developed throughout your lifetime are being tested.

Many of the general questions just described provide all the data needed to answer the questions and ask you to use your reasoning ability to find the answers. Your best preparation for these tests, as well as for tests of facts and ideas, is to be at your physical and mental best. You, no doubt, have your own methods of getting into an exam-taking mood and keeping "in shape." The next section lists some ideas on this subject.

IV. KINDS OF QUESTIONS

Only rarely is the "essay" question, which you answer in narrative form, used in civil service tests. Civil service tests are usually of the short-answer type. Full instructions for answering these questions will be given to you at the examination. But in case this is your first experience with short-answer questions and separate answer sheets, here is what you need to know:

1) Multiple-choice Questions

Most popular of the short-answer questions is the "multiple choice" or "best answer" question. It can be used, for example, to test for factual knowledge, ability to solve problems or judgment in meeting situations found at work.

A multiple-choice question is normally one of three types—
- It can begin with an incomplete statement followed by several possible endings. You are to find the one ending which *best* completes the statement, although some of the others may not be entirely wrong.
- It can also be a complete statement in the form of a question which is answered by choosing one of the statements listed.

- It can be in the form of a problem – again you select the best answer.

Here is an example of a multiple-choice question with a discussion which should give you some clues as to the method for choosing the right answer:

When an employee has a complaint about his assignment, the action which will *best* help him overcome his difficulty is to
  A. discuss his difficulty with his coworkers
  B. take the problem to the head of the organization
  C. take the problem to the person who gave him the assignment
  D. say nothing to anyone about his complaint

In answering this question, you should study each of the choices to find which is best. Consider choice "A" – Certainly an employee may discuss his complaint with fellow employees, but no change or improvement can result, and the complaint remains unresolved. Choice "B" is a poor choice since the head of the organization probably does not know what assignment you have been given, and taking your problem to him is known as "going over the head" of the supervisor. The supervisor, or person who made the assignment, is the person who can clarify it or correct any injustice. Choice "C" is, therefore, correct. To say nothing, as in choice "D," is unwise. Supervisors have and interest in knowing the problems employees are facing, and the employee is seeking a solution to his problem.

2) True/False Questions

The "true/false" or "right/wrong" form of question is sometimes used. Here a complete statement is given. Your job is to decide whether the statement is right or wrong.

SAMPLE: A roaming cell-phone call to a nearby city costs less than a non-roaming call to a distant city.

This statement is wrong, or false, since roaming calls are more expensive.

This is not a complete list of all possible question forms, although most of the others are variations of these common types. You will always get complete directions for answering questions. Be sure you understand *how* to mark your answers – ask questions until you do.

V. RECORDING YOUR ANSWERS

Computer terminals are used more and more today for many different kinds of exams.
For an examination with very few applicants, you may be told to record your answers in the test booklet itself. Separate answer sheets are much more common. If this separate answer sheet is to be scored by machine – and this is often the case – it is highly important that you mark your answers correctly in order to get credit.
An electronic scoring machine is often used in civil service offices because of the speed with which papers can be scored. Machine-scored answer sheets must be marked with a pencil, which will be given to you. This pencil has a high graphite content which responds to the electronic scoring machine. As a matter of fact, stray dots may register as answers, so do not let your pencil rest on the answer sheet while you are pondering the correct answer. Also, if your pencil lead breaks or is otherwise defective, ask for another.

Since the answer sheet will be dropped in a slot in the scoring machine, be careful not to bend the corners or get the paper crumpled.

The answer sheet normally has five vertical columns of numbers, with 30 numbers to a column. These numbers correspond to the question numbers in your test booklet. After each number, going across the page are four or five pairs of dotted lines. These short dotted lines have small letters or numbers above them. The first two pairs may also have a "T" or "F" above the letters. This indicates that the first two pairs only are to be used if the questions are of the true-false type. If the questions are multiple choice, disregard the "T" and "F" and pay attention only to the small letters or numbers.

Answer your questions in the manner of the sample that follows:

32. The largest city in the United States is
    A. Washington, D.C.
    B. New York City
    C. Chicago
    D. Detroit
    E. San Francisco

1) Choose the answer you think is best. (New York City is the largest, so "B" is correct.)
2) Find the row of dotted lines numbered the same as the question you are answering. (Find row number 32)
3) Find the pair of dotted lines corresponding to the answer. (Find the pair of lines under the mark "B.")
4) Make a solid black mark between the dotted lines.

VI. BEFORE THE TEST

Common sense will help you find procedures to follow to get ready for an examination. Too many of us, however, overlook these sensible measures. Indeed, nervousness and fatigue have been found to be the most serious reasons why applicants fail to do their best on civil service tests. Here is a list of reminders:

- Begin your preparation early – Don't wait until the last minute to go scurrying around for books and materials or to find out what the position is all about.
- Prepare continuously – An hour a night for a week is better than an all-night cram session. This has been definitely established. What is more, a night a week for a month will return better dividends than crowding your study into a shorter period of time.
- Locate the place of the exam – You have been sent a notice telling you when and where to report for the examination. If the location is in a different town or otherwise unfamiliar to you, it would be well to inquire the best route and learn something about the building.
- Relax the night before the test – Allow your mind to rest. Do not study at all that night. Plan some mild recreation or diversion; then go to bed early and get a good night's sleep.
- Get up early enough to make a leisurely trip to the place for the test – This way unforeseen events, traffic snarls, unfamiliar buildings, etc. will not upset you.
- Dress comfortably – A written test is not a fashion show. You will be known by number and not by name, so wear something comfortable.

- Leave excess paraphernalia at home – Shopping bags and odd bundles will get in your way. You need bring only the items mentioned in the official notice you received; usually everything you need is provided. Do not bring reference books to the exam. They will only confuse those last minutes and be taken away from you when in the test room.
- Arrive somewhat ahead of time – If because of transportation schedules you must get there very early, bring a newspaper or magazine to take your mind off yourself while waiting.
- Locate the examination room – When you have found the proper room, you will be directed to the seat or part of the room where you will sit. Sometimes you are given a sheet of instructions to read while you are waiting. Do not fill out any forms until you are told to do so; just read them and be prepared.
- Relax and prepare to listen to the instructions
- If you have any physical problem that may keep you from doing your best, be sure to tell the test administrator. If you are sick or in poor health, you really cannot do your best on the exam. You can come back and take the test some other time.

VII. AT THE TEST

The day of the test is here and you have the test booklet in your hand. The temptation to get going is very strong. Caution! There is more to success than knowing the right answers. You must know how to identify your papers and understand variations in the type of short-answer question used in this particular examination. Follow these suggestions for maximum results from your efforts:

1) Cooperate with the monitor

The test administrator has a duty to create a situation in which you can be as much at ease as possible. He will give instructions, tell you when to begin, check to see that you are marking your answer sheet correctly, and so on. He is not there to guard you, although he will see that your competitors do not take unfair advantage. He wants to help you do your best.

2) Listen to all instructions

Don't jump the gun! Wait until you understand all directions. In most civil service tests you get more time than you need to answer the questions. So don't be in a hurry. Read each word of instructions until you clearly understand the meaning. Study the examples, listen to all announcements and follow directions. Ask questions if you do not understand what to do.

3) Identify your papers

Civil service exams are usually identified by number only. You will be assigned a number; you must not put your name on your test papers. Be sure to copy your number correctly. Since more than one exam may be given, copy your exact examination title.

4) Plan your time

Unless you are told that a test is a "speed" or "rate of work" test, speed itself is usually not important. Time enough to answer all the questions will be provided, but this does not mean that you have all day. An overall time limit has been set. Divide the total time (in minutes) by the number of questions to determine the approximate time you have for each question.

5) Do not linger over difficult questions

If you come across a difficult question, mark it with a paper clip (useful to have along) and come back to it when you have been through the booklet. One caution if you do this – be sure to skip a number on your answer sheet as well. Check often to be sure that you have not lost your place and that you are marking in the row numbered the same as the question you are answering.

6) Read the questions

Be sure you know what the question asks! Many capable people are unsuccessful because they failed to *read* the questions correctly.

7) Answer all questions

Unless you have been instructed that a penalty will be deducted for incorrect answers, it is better to guess than to omit a question.

8) Speed tests

It is often better NOT to guess on speed tests. It has been found that on timed tests people are tempted to spend the last few seconds before time is called in marking answers at random – without even reading them – in the hope of picking up a few extra points. To discourage this practice, the instructions may warn you that your score will be "corrected" for guessing. That is, a penalty will be applied. The incorrect answers will be deducted from the correct ones, or some other penalty formula will be used.

9) Review your answers

If you finish before time is called, go back to the questions you guessed or omitted to give them further thought. Review other answers if you have time.

10) Return your test materials

If you are ready to leave before others have finished or time is called, take ALL your materials to the monitor and leave quietly. Never take any test material with you. The monitor can discover whose papers are not complete, and taking a test booklet may be grounds for disqualification.

VIII. EXAMINATION TECHNIQUES

1) Read the general instructions carefully. These are usually printed on the first page of the exam booklet. As a rule, these instructions refer to the timing of the examination; the fact that you should not start work until the signal and must stop work at a signal, etc. If there are any *special* instructions, such as a choice of questions to be answered, make sure that you note this instruction carefully.

2) When you are ready to start work on the examination, that is as soon as the signal has been given, read the instructions to each question booklet, underline any key words or phrases, such as *least, best, outline, describe* and the like. In this way you will tend to answer as requested rather than discover on reviewing your paper that you *listed without describing*, that you selected the *worst* choice rather than the *best* choice, etc.

3) If the examination is of the objective or multiple-choice type – that is, each question will also give a series of possible answers: A, B, C or D, and you are called upon to select the best answer and write the letter next to that answer on your answer paper – it is advisable to start answering each question in turn. There may be anywhere from 50 to 100 such questions in the three or four hours allotted and you can see how much time would be taken if you read through all the questions before beginning to answer any. Furthermore, if you come across a question or group of questions which you know would be difficult to answer, it would undoubtedly affect your handling of all the other questions.

4) If the examination is of the essay type and contains but a few questions, it is a moot point as to whether you should read all the questions before starting to answer any one. Of course, if you are given a choice – say five out of seven and the like – then it is essential to read all the questions so you can eliminate the two that are most difficult. If, however, you are asked to answer all the questions, there may be danger in trying to answer the easiest one first because you may find that you will spend too much time on it. The best technique is to answer the first question, then proceed to the second, etc.

5) Time your answers. Before the exam begins, write down the time it started, then add the time allowed for the examination and write down the time it must be completed, then divide the time available somewhat as follows:
    - If 3-1/2 hours are allowed, that would be 210 minutes. If you have 80 objective-type questions, that would be an average of 2-1/2 minutes per question. Allow yourself no more than 2 minutes per question, or a total of 160 minutes, which will permit about 50 minutes to review.
    - If for the time allotment of 210 minutes there are 7 essay questions to answer, that would average about 30 minutes a question. Give yourself only 25 minutes per question so that you have about 35 minutes to review.

6) The most important instruction is to *read each question* and make sure you know what is wanted. The second most important instruction is to *time yourself properly* so that you answer every question. The third most important instruction is to *answer every question*. Guess if you have to but include something for each question. Remember that you will receive no credit for a blank and will probably receive some credit if you write something in answer to an essay question. If you guess a letter – say "B" for a multiple-choice question – you may have guessed right. If you leave a blank as an answer to a multiple-choice question, the examiners may respect your feelings but it will not add a point to your score. Some exams may penalize you for wrong answers, so in such cases *only*, you may not want to guess unless you have some basis for your answer.

7) Suggestions
    a. Objective-type questions
        1. Examine the question booklet for proper sequence of pages and questions
        2. Read all instructions carefully
        3. Skip any question which seems too difficult; return to it after all other questions have been answered
        4. Apportion your time properly; do not spend too much time on any single question or group of questions

5. Note and underline key words – *all, most, fewest, least, best, worst, same, opposite,* etc.
6. Pay particular attention to negatives
7. Note unusual option, e.g., unduly long, short, complex, different or similar in content to the body of the question
8. Observe the use of "hedging" words – *probably, may, most likely,* etc.
9. Make sure that your answer is put next to the same number as the question
10. Do not second-guess unless you have good reason to believe the second answer is definitely more correct
11. Cross out original answer if you decide another answer is more accurate; do not erase until you are ready to hand your paper in
12. Answer all questions; guess unless instructed otherwise
13. Leave time for review

b. Essay questions
1. Read each question carefully
2. Determine exactly what is wanted. Underline key words or phrases.
3. Decide on outline or paragraph answer
4. Include many different points and elements unless asked to develop any one or two points or elements
5. Show impartiality by giving pros and cons unless directed to select one side only
6. Make and write down any assumptions you find necessary to answer the questions
7. Watch your English, grammar, punctuation and choice of words
8. Time your answers; don't crowd material

8) Answering the essay question

Most essay questions can be answered by framing the specific response around several key words or ideas. Here are a few such key words or ideas:

M's: manpower, materials, methods, money, management
P's: purpose, program, policy, plan, procedure, practice, problems, pitfalls, personnel, public relations

  a. Six basic steps in handling problems:
  1. Preliminary plan and background development
  2. Collect information, data and facts
  3. Analyze and interpret information, data and facts
  4. Analyze and develop solutions as well as make recommendations
  5. Prepare report and sell recommendations
  6. Install recommendations and follow up effectiveness

  b. Pitfalls to avoid
  1. *Taking things for granted* – A statement of the situation does not necessarily imply that each of the elements is necessarily true; for example, a complaint may be invalid and biased so that all that can be taken for granted is that a complaint has been registered

2. *Considering only one side of a situation* – Wherever possible, indicate several alternatives and then point out the reasons you selected the best one
3. *Failing to indicate follow up* – Whenever your answer indicates action on your part, make certain that you will take proper follow-up action to see how successful your recommendations, procedures or actions turn out to be
4. *Taking too long in answering any single question* – Remember to time your answers properly

IX. AFTER THE TEST

Scoring procedures differ in detail among civil service jurisdictions although the general principles are the same. Whether the papers are hand-scored or graded by machine we have described, they are nearly always graded by number. That is, the person who marks the paper knows only the number – never the name – of the applicant. Not until all the papers have been graded will they be matched with names. If other tests, such as training and experience or oral interview ratings have been given, scores will be combined. Different parts of the examination usually have different weights. For example, the written test might count 60 percent of the final grade, and a rating of training and experience 40 percent. In many jurisdictions, veterans will have a certain number of points added to their grades.

After the final grade has been determined, the names are placed in grade order and an eligible list is established. There are various methods for resolving ties between those who get the same final grade – probably the most common is to place first the name of the person whose application was received first. Job offers are made from the eligible list in the order the names appear on it. You will be notified of your grade and your rank as soon as all these computations have been made. This will be done as rapidly as possible.

People who are found to meet the requirements in the announcement are called "eligibles." Their names are put on a list of eligible candidates. An eligible's chances of getting a job depend on how high he stands on this list and how fast agencies are filling jobs from the list.

When a job is to be filled from a list of eligibles, the agency asks for the names of people on the list of eligibles for that job. When the civil service commission receives this request, it sends to the agency the names of the three people highest on this list. Or, if the job to be filled has specialized requirements, the office sends the agency the names of the top three persons who meet these requirements from the general list.

The appointing officer makes a choice from among the three people whose names were sent to him. If the selected person accepts the appointment, the names of the others are put back on the list to be considered for future openings.

That is the rule in hiring from all kinds of eligible lists, whether they are for typist, carpenter, chemist, or something else. For every vacancy, the appointing officer has his choice of any one of the top three eligibles on the list. This explains why the person whose name is on top of the list sometimes does not get an appointment when some of the persons lower on the list do. If the appointing officer chooses the second or third eligible, the No. 1 eligible does not get a job at once, but stays on the list until he is appointed or the list is terminated.

X. HOW TO PASS THE INTERVIEW TEST

The examination for which you applied requires an oral interview test. You have already taken the written test and you are now being called for the interview test – the final part of the formal examination.

You may think that it is not possible to prepare for an interview test and that there are no procedures to follow during an interview. Our purpose is to point out some things you can do in advance that will help you and some good rules to follow and pitfalls to avoid while you are being interviewed.

What is an interview supposed to test?

The written examination is designed to test the technical knowledge and competence of the candidate; the oral is designed to evaluate intangible qualities, not readily measured otherwise, and to establish a list showing the relative fitness of each candidate – as measured against his competitors – for the position sought. Scoring is not on the basis of "right" and "wrong," but on a sliding scale of values ranging from "not passable" to "outstanding." As a matter of fact, it is possible to achieve a relatively low score without a single "incorrect" answer because of evident weakness in the qualities being measured.

Occasionally, an examination may consist entirely of an oral test – either an individual or a group oral. In such cases, information is sought concerning the technical knowledges and abilities of the candidate, since there has been no written examination for this purpose. More commonly, however, an oral test is used to supplement a written examination.

Who conducts interviews?

The composition of oral boards varies among different jurisdictions. In nearly all, a representative of the personnel department serves as chairman. One of the members of the board may be a representative of the department in which the candidate would work. In some cases, "outside experts" are used, and, frequently, a businessman or some other representative of the general public is asked to serve. Labor and management or other special groups may be represented. The aim is to secure the services of experts in the appropriate field.

However the board is composed, it is a good idea (and not at all improper or unethical) to ascertain in advance of the interview who the members are and what groups they represent. When you are introduced to them, you will have some idea of their backgrounds and interests, and at least you will not stutter and stammer over their names.

What should be done before the interview?

While knowledge about the board members is useful and takes some of the surprise element out of the interview, there is other preparation which is more substantive. It *is* possible to prepare for an oral interview – in several ways:

1) Keep a copy of your application and review it carefully before the interview

This may be the only document before the oral board, and the starting point of the interview. Know what education and experience you have listed there, and the sequence and dates of all of it. Sometimes the board will ask you to review the highlights of your experience for them; you should not have to hem and haw doing it.

2) Study the class specification and the examination announcement

Usually, the oral board has one or both of these to guide them. The qualities, characteristics or knowledges required by the position sought are stated in these documents. They offer valuable clues as to the nature of the oral interview. For example, if the job involves supervisory responsibilities, the announcement will usually indicate that knowledge of modern supervisory methods and the qualifications of the candidate as a supervisor will be tested. If so, you can expect such questions, frequently in the form of a hypothetical situation which you are expected to solve. NEVER go into an oral without knowledge of the duties and responsibilities of the job you seek.

3) Think through each qualification required

Try to visualize the kind of questions you would ask if you were a board member. How well could you answer them? Try especially to appraise your own knowledge and background in each area, *measured against the job sought*, and identify any areas in which you are weak. Be critical and realistic – do not flatter yourself.

4) Do some general reading in areas in which you feel you may be weak

For example, if the job involves supervision and your past experience has NOT, some general reading in supervisory methods and practices, particularly in the field of human relations, might be useful. Do NOT study agency procedures or detailed manuals. The oral board will be testing your understanding and capacity, not your memory.

5) Get a good night's sleep and watch your general health and mental attitude

You will want a clear head at the interview. Take care of a cold or any other minor ailment, and of course, no hangovers.

What should be done on the day of the interview?

Now comes the day of the interview itself. Give yourself plenty of time to get there. Plan to arrive somewhat ahead of the scheduled time, particularly if your appointment is in the fore part of the day. If a previous candidate fails to appear, the board might be ready for you a bit early. By early afternoon an oral board is almost invariably behind schedule if there are many candidates, and you may have to wait. Take along a book or magazine to read, or your application to review, but leave any extraneous material in the waiting room when you go in for your interview. In any event, relax and compose yourself.

The matter of dress is important. The board is forming impressions about you – from your experience, your manners, your attitude, and your appearance. Give your personal appearance careful attention. Dress your best, but not your flashiest. Choose conservative, appropriate clothing, and be sure it is immaculate. This is a business interview, and your appearance should indicate that you regard it as such. Besides, being well groomed and properly dressed will help boost your confidence.

Sooner or later, someone will call your name and escort you into the interview room. *This is it.* From here on you are on your own. It is too late for any more preparation. But remember, you asked for this opportunity to prove your fitness, and you are here because your request was granted.

What happens when you go in?

The usual sequence of events will be as follows: The clerk (who is often the board stenographer) will introduce you to the chairman of the oral board, who will introduce you to the other members of the board. Acknowledge the introductions before you sit down. Do not be surprised if you find a microphone facing you or a stenotypist sitting by. Oral interviews are usually recorded in the event of an appeal or other review.

Usually the chairman of the board will open the interview by reviewing the highlights of your education and work experience from your application – primarily for the benefit of the other members of the board, as well as to get the material into the record. Do not interrupt or comment unless there is an error or significant misinterpretation; if that is the case, do not hesitate. But do not quibble about insignificant matters. Also, he will usually ask you some question about your education, experience or your present job – partly to get you to start talking and to establish the interviewing "rapport." He may start the actual questioning, or turn it over to one of the other members. Frequently, each member undertakes the questioning on a particular area, one in which he is perhaps most competent, so you can expect each member to participate in the examination. Because time is limited, you may also expect some rather abrupt switches in the direction the questioning takes, so do not be upset by it. Normally, a board member will not pursue a single line of questioning unless he discovers a particular strength or weakness.

After each member has participated, the chairman will usually ask whether any member has any further questions, then will ask you if you have anything you wish to add. Unless you are expecting this question, it may floor you. Worse, it may start you off on an extended, extemporaneous speech. The board is not usually seeking more information. The question is principally to offer you a last opportunity to present further qualifications or to indicate that you have nothing to add. So, if you feel that a significant qualification or characteristic has been overlooked, it is proper to point it out in a sentence or so. Do not compliment the board on the thoroughness of their examination – they have been sketchy, and you know it. If you wish, merely say, "No thank you, I have nothing further to add." This is a point where you can "talk yourself out" of a good impression or fail to present an important bit of information. Remember, *you close the interview yourself*.

The chairman will then say, "That is all, Mr. _____, thank you." Do not be startled; the interview is over, and quicker than you think. Thank him, gather your belongings and take your leave. Save your sigh of relief for the other side of the door.

How to put your best foot forward

Throughout this entire process, you may feel that the board individually and collectively is trying to pierce your defenses, seek out your hidden weaknesses and embarrass and confuse you. Actually, this is not true. They are obliged to make an appraisal of your qualifications for the job you are seeking, and they want to see you in your best light. Remember, they must interview all candidates and a non-cooperative candidate may become a failure in spite of their best efforts to bring out his qualifications. Here are 15 suggestions that will help you:

1) Be natural – Keep your attitude confident, not cocky

If you are not confident that you can do the job, do not expect the board to be. Do not apologize for your weaknesses, try to bring out your strong points. The board is interested in a positive, not negative, presentation. Cockiness will antagonize any board member and make him wonder if you are covering up a weakness by a false show of strength.

2) Get comfortable, but don't lounge or sprawl

Sit erectly but not stiffly. A careless posture may lead the board to conclude that you are careless in other things, or at least that you are not impressed by the importance of the occasion. Either conclusion is natural, even if incorrect. Do not fuss with your clothing, a pencil or an ashtray. Your hands may occasionally be useful to emphasize a point; do not let them become a point of distraction.

3) Do not wisecrack or make small talk

This is a serious situation, and your attitude should show that you consider it as such. Further, the time of the board is limited – they do not want to waste it, and neither should you.

4) Do not exaggerate your experience or abilities

In the first place, from information in the application or other interviews and sources, the board may know more about you than you think. Secondly, you probably will not get away with it. An experienced board is rather adept at spotting such a situation, so do not take the chance.

5) If you know a board member, do not make a point of it, yet do not hide it

Certainly you are not fooling him, and probably not the other members of the board. Do not try to take advantage of your acquaintanceship – it will probably do you little good.

6) Do not dominate the interview

Let the board do that. They will give you the clues – do not assume that you have to do all the talking. Realize that the board has a number of questions to ask you, and do not try to take up all the interview time by showing off your extensive knowledge of the answer to the first one.

7) Be attentive

You only have 20 minutes or so, and you should keep your attention at its sharpest throughout. When a member is addressing a problem or question to you, give him your undivided attention. Address your reply principally to him, but do not exclude the other board members.

8) Do not interrupt

A board member may be stating a problem for you to analyze. He will ask you a question when the time comes. Let him state the problem, and wait for the question.

9) Make sure you understand the question

Do not try to answer until you are sure what the question is. If it is not clear, restate it in your own words or ask the board member to clarify it for you. However, do not haggle about minor elements.

10) Reply promptly but not hastily

A common entry on oral board rating sheets is "candidate responded readily," or "candidate hesitated in replies." Respond as promptly and quickly as you can, but do not jump to a hasty, ill-considered answer.

11) Do not be peremptory in your answers

A brief answer is proper – but do not fire your answer back. That is a losing game from your point of view. The board member can probably ask questions much faster than you can answer them.

12) Do not try to create the answer you think the board member wants

He is interested in what kind of mind you have and how it works – not in playing games. Furthermore, he can usually spot this practice and will actually grade you down on it.

13) Do not switch sides in your reply merely to agree with a board member

Frequently, a member will take a contrary position merely to draw you out and to see if you are willing and able to defend your point of view. Do not start a debate, yet do not surrender a good position. If a position is worth taking, it is worth defending.

14) Do not be afraid to admit an error in judgment if you are shown to be wrong

The board knows that you are forced to reply without any opportunity for careful consideration. Your answer may be demonstrably wrong. If so, admit it and get on with the interview.

15) Do not dwell at length on your present job

The opening question may relate to your present assignment. Answer the question but do not go into an extended discussion. You are being examined for a *new* job, not your present one. As a matter of fact, try to phrase ALL your answers in terms of the job for which you are being examined.

Basis of Rating

Probably you will forget most of these "do's" and "don'ts" when you walk into the oral interview room. Even remembering them all will not ensure you a passing grade. Perhaps you did not have the qualifications in the first place. But remembering them will help you to put your best foot forward, without treading on the toes of the board members.

Rumor and popular opinion to the contrary notwithstanding, an oral board wants you to make the best appearance possible. They know you are under pressure – but they also want to see how you respond to it as a guide to what your reaction would be under the pressures of the job you seek. They will be influenced by the degree of poise you display, the personal traits you show and the manner in which you respond.

ABOUT THIS BOOK

This book contains tests divided into Examination Sections. Go through each test, answering every question in the margin. We have also attached a sample answer sheet at the back of the book that can be removed and used. At the end of each test look at the answer key and check your answers. On the ones you got wrong, look at the right answer choice and learn. Do not fill in the answers first. Do not memorize the questions and answers, but understand the answer and principles involved. On your test, the questions will likely be different from the samples. Questions are changed and new ones added. If you understand these past questions you should have success with any changes that arise. Tests may consist of several types of questions. We have additional books on each subject should more study be advisable or necessary for you. Finally, the more you study, the better prepared you will be. This book is intended to be the last thing you study before you walk into the examination room. Prior study of relevant texts is also recommended. NLC publishes some of these in our Fundamental Series. Knowledge and good sense are important factors in passing your exam. Good luck also helps. So now study this Passbook, absorb the material contained within and take that knowledge into the examination. Then do your best to pass that exam.

EXAMINATION SECTION

EXAMINATION SECTION
TEST 1

DIRECTIONS: Each question or incomplete statement is followed by several suggested answers or completions. Select the one that BEST answers the question or completes the statement. *PRINT THE LETTER OF THE CORRECT ANSWER IN THE SPACE AT THE RIGHT.*

1. Of the following methods of installing pipe in a trench, the one which is MOST acceptable is to

   A. use a flat bottom trench and backfill not tamped
   B. have pipe supported on blocks and backfill tamped
   C. use a flat bottom trench and backfill tamped
   D. have pipe supported on blocks, backfill not tamped

   1.____

2. When cutting a 30" diameter cast iron pipe, it is BEST to use a(n)

   A. cold chisel
   B. diamond point chisel
   C. hardy
   D. ordinary wheel type of cutter

   2.____

3. Of the following materials, the one which is BEST suited for yarning bell and spigot joints on water pipe is

   A. plumber's yarn
   B. boatmaker's yarn
   C. tar impregnated oakum
   D. sterilized yarn

   3.____

4. A valve that is used between low pressure and high pressure areas in water distribution systems is called a boundary valve.

   A. pressure reducing
   B. check
   C. gate
   D. globe

   4.____

5. Cast iron pipe is particularly adapted to underground and submerged service because of its

   A. ease in handling and joining
   B. high corrosion-resisting qualities
   C. ability to withstand high pressures
   D. low first cost

   5.____

6. In caulking a pipe joint, excessive *caulking* should be avoided to prevent

   A. *thinning* the lead
   B. a second pouring of lead
   C. *misses*
   D. bell damage

   6.____

7. The material used to disinfect water pipes before and after laying the pipe is USUALLY

   A. chlordane
   B. calcium chloride
   C. chlorine
   D. washing soda

   7.____

1

8. Of the following items, the one that is NOT a component part of a mechanical joint is a(n) 8._____
   A. yarn B. gland
   C. rubber gasket D. socket

9. Of the following causes of water leaks in mains, the one that is LEAST common is 9._____
   A. improper caulking
   B. poor backfilling
   C. improper handling of pipe
   D. manufacturing defects in the pipe

10. The BEST type of wrench to use for making up a mechanical joint in cast iron pipe is a _____ wrench. 10._____
    A. ratchet B. monkey C. strap D. Stillson

11. The MAIN difference between skeleton sheathing and tight sheathing is that in skeleton sheathing 11._____
    A. a greater part of the sheathing is omitted
    B. reinforced laced type of sheathing is used
    C. the rangers and braces are placed differently
    D. no planks are used

12. The width of the trench at each caulking joint, in comparison with the remaining portion of the trench, should generally be 12._____
    A. equal to twice the diameter of the pipe to allow for caulking
    B. of sufficient size to allow for caulking
    C. equal to the diameter of the pipe plus 12 inches
    D. equal to the diameter of the pipe plus 1/2 pipe radius

13. Unless otherwise directed, a trench for a water pipe line should USUALLY be excavated to a depth of 4 feet measured from the surface of the roadway to the _____ of the pipe. 13._____
    A. center B. bottom C. invert D. top

14. The length of trench excavation for the installation of a 30-inch pipe should NOT exceed _____ feet. 14._____
    A. 1500 B. 1300 C. 1100 D. 1000

15. Before laying a new water main, test pits or test trenches may be necessary in order to determine 15._____
    A. the amount of materials required
    B. subsurface obstructions
    C. the proper width of excavation
    D. the amount of labor needed

16. The outside circumference of a pipe that has an outside diameter of 11 1/2" is MOST NEARLY 16._____
    A. 32" B. 36" C. 39" D. 42"

17. Continuous sheathing is USUALLY used when excavating a trench in

    A. unstable soil B. firm earth
    C. stiff clay   D. rock

18. Assume that a pump is pumping water out of an excavated trench at the rate of 30 gallons per minute.
    The time that is required to pump 2700 gallons of water out of this trench would be MOST NEARLY _____ hour(s).

    A. 4 1/2   B. 3   C. 1 1/2   D. 3/4

19. The size of *rangers* that should be used for trenches dug to a depth of seven (7) feet is APPROXIMATELY

    A. 1" x 2"   B. 2" x 3"   C. 2" x 4"   D. 4" x 6"

20. The bottom of wood sheathing is USUALLY

    A. squared on all sides
    B. steel tipped in order to penetrate hard material
    C. capped in order to prevent splintering
    D. bevelled on both one face and one edge

21. The quickest and easiest way of disconnecting a bell and spigot lead joint in a pipe is by

    A. using a picking chisel at the joint
    B. cracking the bell
    C. melting the lead at the joint with an acetylene torch
    D. using a diamond point chisel

22. A joint runner is USUALLY used as a

    A. guide for molten lead
    B. scab on sheathing
    C. clamp for two pipes
    D. filler between pavement joints

23. Of the following tools, the one which is NOT usually used for caulking a joint is the

    A. stub   B. regular
    C. cold chisel D. diamond joint

24. The type of lead USUALLY used to caulk cast iron pipe joints in water mains is

    A. lead wool B. shredded lead
    C. leadite   D. pure soft lead

25. The distance that a *ranger* is USUALLY placed below the surface of a roadway is APPROXIMATELY

    A. 12"   B. 10"   C. 8"   D. 6"

26. The proper manner to unload cast iron pipe at a trench site which is APPROXIMATELY 300 feet long is to

    A. stack it at convenient locations
    B. stack it in even layers with 4" x 4" stringers between each layer with blocks at each end
    C. lay it along the route with the bell facing in the direction in which the work is to proceed
    D. store it where it will not collect rain water and be damaged in freezing weather

27. Damage to cast iron pipe may sometimes result from rough handling when in transit. A simple method of determining whether the pipe was damaged or not is to

    A. *ring* each length with a hammer
    B. drop the pipe to see if it breaks
    C. hydraulically test the pipe
    D. visually examine the pipe for cracks

28. A blowoff connection in a water distribution main is USUALLY located at the

    A. highest point of the line
    B. lowest point of the line
    C. midway point between two distribution mains
    D. center line of the pipe

29. The proper depth of lead joints for a 4" or 6" cast iron pipe is MOST NEARLY _____ inches.

    A. 3 1/2   B. 3 1/4   C. 3   D. 2 3/8

30. The distance that fire hydrants should be located back from the face of the curb line is MOST NEARLY

    A. 6-10"   B. 12-16"   C. 18-20"   D. 22-26"

31. Your orders to your crew are MOST likely to be followed if you

    A. explain the reasons for these orders
    B. warn that all violators will be punished
    C. promise easy assignments to those who follow these orders best
    D. say that they are for the good of the department

32. In order to be a good supervisor, you should

    A. impress upon your men that you demand perfection in their work at all times
    B. avoid being blamed for your crew's mistakes
    C. impress your superior with your ability
    D. see to it that your men get what they are entitled to

33. In giving instructions to a crew, you should

    A. speak in as loud a tone as possible
    B. speak in a coaxing persuasive manner
    C. speak quietly, clearly, and courteously
    D. always use the word *please* when giving instructions

34. The BEST procedure to follow when a difficult and unusual problem arises involving the laying of a water pipe is to

    A. ask another pipe caulker for his opinion
    B. proceed working in the usual manner
    C. report the situation to the engineer
    D. continue working, making necessary changes yourself

35. Assume that you are in charge of a crew making repairs on a water main. A bystander whom you do not know begins to comment on the way the work is being done. He makes several suggestions which he claims will result in a better job.
    Of the following, you should

    A. hold up the work until you can discuss the suggestions with your superior
    B. listen to him, thank him, and proceed with the work as you have been doing
    C. tell him to go along about his own business since you can do the job without any advice
    D. tell him to take his comments and suggestions to your superior who has the authority to change procedure

36. Assume that a pipe worker earns $16,625 per year. If seventeen percent of his pay is deducted for taxes, social security, and pension, his net weekly pay will be APPROXIMATELY

    A. $319.70   B. $300.80   C. $290.60   D. $265.00

37. If eighteen (18) feet of 4" cast iron pipe weighs approximately 390 pounds, the weight of this pipe per lineal foot will be MOST NEARLY _____ lbs.

    A. 19   B. 21   C. 23   D. 25

38. A one-sixteenth cast iron fitting will change the direction of water APPROXIMATELY

    A. 90°   B. 45°   C. 22 1/2°   D. 11 1/4°

39. The overall length of a standard cast iron bell-and-spigot water pipe is MOST NEARLY

    A. 10' 4 1/2"   B. 11'9"   C. 12' 4 1/2"   D. 20'0"

40. In rock excavations, the minimum depth that rock must be removed from the bottom of the bell of a cast iron pipe to the bottom of a trench should be MOST NEARLY

    A. 3"   B. 4"   C. 6"   D. 9"

KEY (CORRECT ANSWERS)

1. C	11. A	21. C	31. A
2. B	12. B	22. A	32. D
3. D	13. D	23. D	33. C
4. C	14. D	24. D	34. C
5. B	15. B	25. A	35. B
6. D	16. B	26. C	36. D
7. C	17. A	27. A	37. B
8. A	18. C	28. B	38. C
9. D	19. D	29. D	39. C
10. A	20. D	30. C	40. C

TEST 2

DIRECTIONS: Each question or incomplete statement is followed by several suggested answers or completions. Select the one that BEST answers the question or completes the statement. *PRINT THE LETTER OF THE CORRECT ANSWER IN THE SPACE AT THE RIGHT.*

1. If four (4) men are *backfilling* a trench, the proper number of men for *tamping* should usually be NOT LESS than   1.____

    A. 2   B. 4   C. 6   D. 8

2. A subsurface leak in a street main may be located by means of a(n)   2.____

    A. amprobe   B. aquaphone
    C. aqueduct   D. drill rod

3. The FIRST step in shutting off a water main in a street is to   3.____

    A. close the blowoff and notify the Department of Public Works
    B. close the blowoff and notify the Police Department
    C. notify the householders and the Fire Department
    D. close the head gates and notify the Fire Department

4. Concentric reducers are used for   4.____

    A. maintaining the same center line elevation
    B. keeping the bottom of the pipe at the same level
    C. changing the direction of flow in a pipe
    D. lowering the inverts of the pipe

5. A valve box is generally built with an open bottom so that   5.____

    A. the valve box can rest directly on the pipe
    B. the valve can be removed rapidly
    C. any water seeping into it will drain away
    D. a bottom connection can be made

6. If lead that is being used for caulking is overheated, it will be found that the caulked lead ring from a joint would MOST likely be   6.____

    A. too soft   B. porous   C. brittle   D. flexible

7. A pipe compound used for making up threaded joints USUALLY acts as a filler between the threads and also as a   7.____

    A. hardener   B. lubricant
    C. cleanser   D. coolant

8. By referring to a concrete mix having a ratio of 1:2:4 is meant that the ingredients are made up of 1 part _____, 2 parts _____, and 4 parts _____.   8.____

    A. cement; sand; gravel   B. sand; cement; water
    C. gravel; sand; cement   D. sand; cement; gravel

9. The total weight of materials (lead and hemp) used in caulking an 8" bell and spigot joint for water is MOST NEARLY _____ lbs.

   A. 7   B. 10   C. 15   D. 24

10. Assume that a length of cast iron pipe measures 9'8" and three pieces of pipe are to be cut from this pipe, one 2'9", the second 3'2", and the third 1'10".
    The amount of pipe remaining after making these cuts (assuming no waste) is MOST NEARLY

    A. 1'6"   B. 1'9"   C. 1'11"   D. 2'2"

11. Of the following types of valves, the one that is used to permit the flow of water in one direction is the _____ valve.

    A. gate   B. angle   C. globe   D. check

12. Water mains in the city are generally located APPROXIMATELY _____ feet from the _____ line.

    A. four (4); curb
    B. five (5); sewer
    C. six (6); building
    D. nine (9); curb

13. Of the following equipment, the one which a pipe worker is NOT normally required to know how to operate is the

    A. backhoe
    B. air-powered chipping hammers and caulking tools
    C. various types of pipe laying derricks
    D. air-powered pavement breakers and rock drills

14. Assume that, after installing a mechanical joint in a water main, a leak occurs around the joint.
    Of the following, the BEST practice to follow would be to

    A. retighten the bolts
    B. loosen the bolts to expand the rubber gasket
    C. *hammer* home the spigot into the bell
    D. disassemble the joint, clean thoroughly, and reassemble

15. It is a good policy to keep excavated material away from the edge of a trench a distance of AT LEAST

    A. 2 feet   B. 18 inches   C. 1 foot   D. 6 inches

16. Neglecting friction, the height, in feet, to which water can rise having a pressure of 55 pounds per square inch is MOST NEARLY

    A. 120   B. 150   C. 180   D. 210

17. If it takes 3 men 11 days to dig a trench, the number of days it will take 5 men to dig the same trench, assuming all work is done at the same rate of speed, is MOST NEARLY

    A. 6 1/2   B. 7 3/4   C. 8 1/4   D. 8 3/4

18. It is sometimes found that poured lead joints tend to crack open due to shrinkage. 18.____
    This is USUALLY due to

    A. overheating of the lead
    B. impurities in the lead
    C. excessive pressure at the joint
    D. cooling of the lead

19. The BEST material to use for backfilling trenches that are made in rock is USUALLY 19.____

    A. tan bark   B. cinders   C. gravel   D. sand

20. For an average pipe repair job, it is the practice to use a gang made up of 20.____

    A. one pipe caulker and three laborers
    B. two pipe caulkers and three laborers
    C. one supervisor, two pipe caulkers, and two laborers
    D. three laborers and two helpers

21. Slack in cables or tie rods is USUALLY *taken up* by the use of 21.____

    A. drift pins   B. clamps
    C. Crosby clips   D. turnbuckles

22. A pneumatic tool is one that is USUALLY directly operated by means of 22.____

    A. gasoline   B. compressed air
    C. oil pressure   D. electricity

23. The BEST thing to do when a pavement breaker becomes jammed in the pavement is to 23.____

    A. attempt to work it loose without using another breaker
    B. shut off the air compressor
    C. increase the air supply
    D. use another pavement breaker to cut it loose

24. If a trench is dug 6'0" deep, 2'6" wide, and 8'0" long, the area of the opening, in square 24.____
    feet, is MOST NEARLY

    A. 48   B. 32   C. 20   D. 15

Questions 25-30.

DIRECTIONS: Questions 25 through 30 are to be answered in accordance with the sketch shown on the following page, which represents a portion of a water distribution map and other facilities.

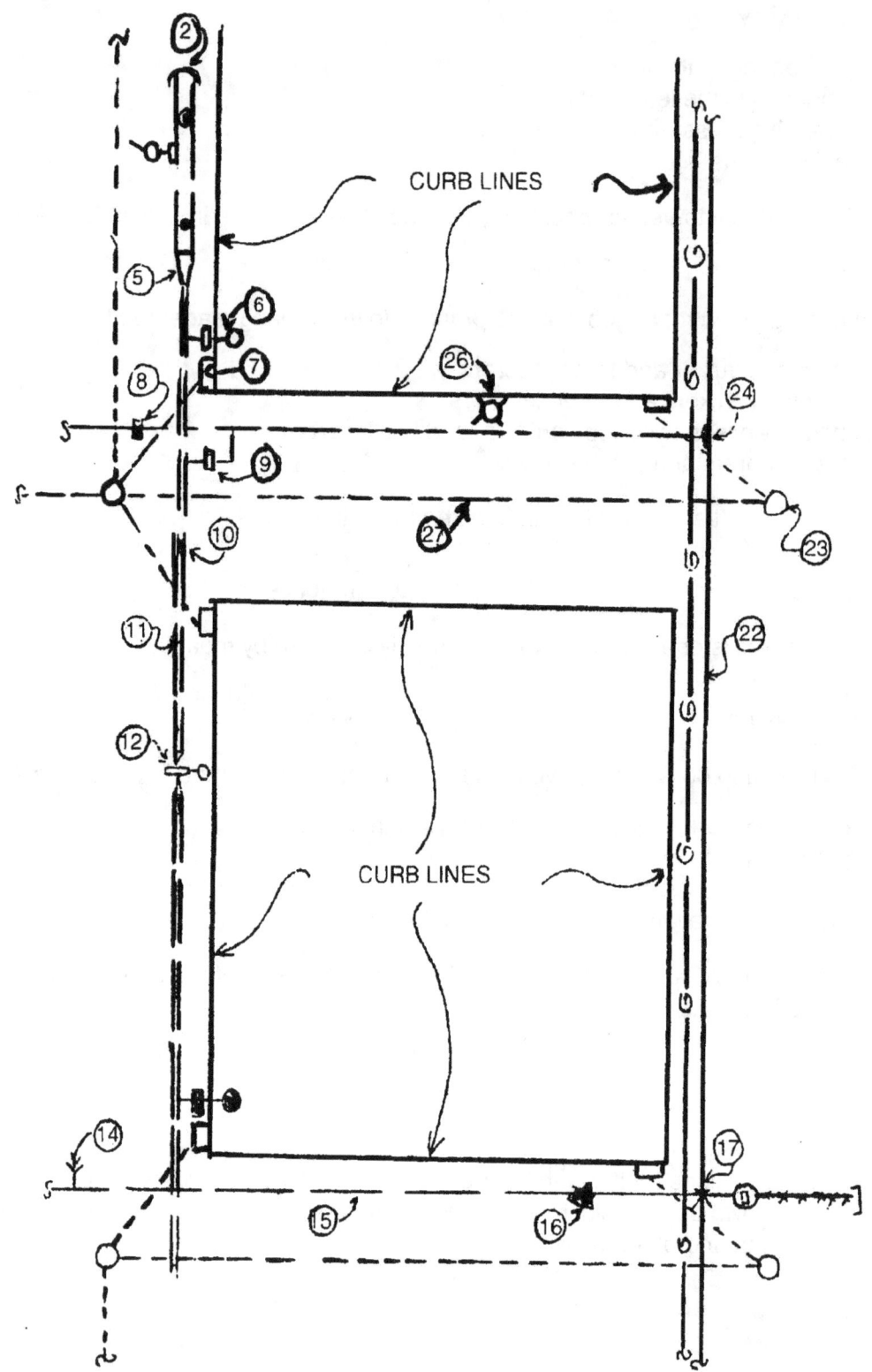

The above sketch represents a portion of a water distribution map and other facilities. To be used in answering questions numbered 25 to 30 inclusive.

25. A hydrant symbol is numbered 25.____
    A. 26   B. 14   C. 6   D. 9

26. A cap symbol is numbered 26.____
    A. 2   B. 5   C. 9   D. 10

27. Of the following numbered lines, the one which is NOT a water line is numbered 27.____
    A. 11   B. 15   C. 22   D. 27

28. A reducer symbol is numbered 28.____
    A. 8   B. 16   C. 12   D. 14

29. A catch basin symbol is numbered 29.____
    A. 7   B. 10   C. 23   D. 24

30. A valve symbol is numbered 30.____
    A. 17   B. 14   C. 10   D. 8

31. Opening a fire hydrant near the high point of a newly installed portion of a water main, prior to testing, is USUALLY done in order to remove 31.____
    A. air
    B. obstructions
    C. slime growths
    D. P. mineral deposits

32. Taps, or wet connections to a city main, may be made by 32.____
    A. a licensed plumber
    B. the Department of Water Supply, Gas and Electricity
    C. the Department of Public Works
    D. any experienced laborer

33. The supervisor made a ridiculous statement. As used in this sentence, the word ridiculous means MOST NEARLY 33.____
    A. incorrect   B. evil   C. unfriendly   D. foolish

34. That pipe caulker is engaged in a hazardous job. As used in this sentence, the word hazardous means MOST NEARLY 34.____
    A. inconvenient
    B. dangerous
    C. difficult
    D. demanding

35. Breaks in water distribution mains are front page news for the very reason that they occur infrequently. As used in this sentence, the word infrequently means MOST NEARLY 35.____
    A. at regular intervals
    B. often
    C. rarely
    D. unexpectedly

36. Several kinds of self-caulking substitutes for lead have been developed. As used in this sentence, the word substitutes means MOST NEARLY 36.____
    A. additives
    B. replacements
    C. hardeners
    D. softeners

37. Cast iron is <u>essentially</u> an alloy of iron and carbon. As used in this sentence, the word <u>essentially</u> means MOST NEARLY   37.____

    A. never   B. basically   C. barely   D. sometimes

38. A pipe worker sometimes makes a <u>trivial</u> mistake. As used in this sentence, the word <u>trivial</u> means MOST NEARLY   38.____

    A. common
    C. obvious
    B. significant
    D. unimportant

39. When water moves through pipe, <u>friction</u> is developed between the water and the inside surface of the pipe. As used in this sentence, the word <u>friction</u> means MOST NEARLY   39.____

    A. resistance
    C. slippage
    B. heat
    D. pressure

40. Assume that a piece of cast iron pipe has to be cut to fit between two cast iron bells fixed in place in a trench. Of the following statements, the one which is MOST NEARLY correct is that, if the pipe is cut too   40.____

    A. short, the next joint may have to be broken to make up the difference
    B. short, the yarn used for caulking might be pushed through past the end of the pipe
    C. long, the proper amount of caulking lead could not be used at the joints
    D. long, the joint would need a bottom support

KEY (CORRECT ANSWERS)

1. B	11. D	21. D	31. A
2. B	12. D	22. B	32. B
3. C	13. A	23. D	33. D
4. A	14. D	24. C	34. B
5. C	15. A	25. C	35. C
6. C	16. A	26. A	36. B
7. B	17. A	27. D	37. B
8. A	18. D	28. B	38. D
9. C	19. D	29. A	39. A
10. C	20. A	30. D	40. B

EXAMINATION SECTION
TEST 1

DIRECTIONS: Each question or incomplete statement is followed by several suggested answers or completions. Select the one that BEST answers the question or completes the statement. *PRINT THE LETTER OF THE CORRECT ANSWER IN THE SPACE AT THE RIGHT.*

1. It is usually necessary to insulate the hot water riser from the cold water riser when the distance between the two risers is

    A. 4" B. 7" C. 9" D. 11"

    1.____

2. The number of threads per inch of 3/4" pipe, as compared with the number of threads per inch of 1/4" pipe, is that the

    A. 3/4" pipe has less threads per inch than 1 1/4" pipe
    B. 3/4" pipe and 1 1/4" pipe have the same number of threads per inch
    C. 1 1/4" pipe has less threads per inch than the 3/4" pipe
    D. 1 1/4" pipe has more threads per inch than 3/4" pipe.

    2.____

3. In comparing the volume of water flowing through 1/2" I.D. tubing line and a 1" I.D. tubing line with the same pressure in each line, the volume through the

    A. 1/2" tubing and the 1" tubing will be the same
    B. 1" tubing will be double the volume of the 1/2" tubing
    C. 1" tubing will be three times the volume of the 1/2" tubing
    D. 1" tubing will be four times the volume of the 1/2" tubing

    3.____

4. Pressure relief valves must be installed on hot water heaters.
   The reason for this is

    A. to drain water from the tank for repair
    B. that when pressure becomes excessive, the relief valve will open and reduce the pressure
    C. that water will be released when tank is full
    D. to prevent air pockets from forming at the bottom of the tank

    4.____

5. The plumbing code requires that water service piping be buried at least four feet below outside ground level. The reason for this is to

    A. prevent the water in the pipe from freezing during the winter season
    B. permit gas service lines to be installed two feet below outside ground level
    C. permit the use of larger diameter pipes
    D. keep the water cool the year round

    5.____

6. A building drain which is buried under ground may NOT be made of

    A. extra heavy cast iron   B. brass
    C. galvanized steel   D. lead

    6.____

7. Brass is an alloy of

    A. lead and copper   B. tin and copper
    C. lead and tin   D. zinc and copper

    7.____

13

8. The MAIN reason for providing a trap for a plumbing fixture is to

   A. permit cleaning of the fixture when clogged
   B. equalize the pressure in the system
   C. prevent the passage of gases in a reverse direction
   D. catch foreign objects such as jewelry, hair pins, etc.

9. The pipe which delivers water under pressure from a street main to a building is called the _____ pipe.

   A. service   B. interceptor
   C. distribution   D. fixture

10. The MAIN reason that a trap must be properly ventilated is to

    A. vary the pressure in the waste line
    B. provide an overflow for the fixture
    C. drain the waste water when the trap is closed
    D. maintain the water seal in the trap

11. The valve which offers the LEAST resistance to water flow in a plumbing system is a(n) _____ valve.

    A. angle   B. gate   C. check   D. globe

12. Outlets for gas ranges must have a MINIMUM standard pipe size of

    A. 1/4"   B. 3/8"   C. 3/4"   D. 1"

13. The oakum for a caulked joint is packed into place by ramming it down with a

    A. yarning iron   B. jointer
    C. caulking tool   D. cold chisel

14. The ESSENTIAL difference in making up vertical and horizontal caulked joints in cast iron pipe is that horizontal caulked joints require the use of

    A. less lead   B. less oakum
    C. a pouring rope   D. a special caulking tool

15. Galvanized pipe has a coating of

    A. tin   B. zinc   C. lead   D. aluminum

16. A fixture unit has a discharge rate of one cubic foot of water per minute. This discharge rate, expressed in gallons per minute, is equal to

    A. 4.5   B. 5   C. 7.5   D. 9.5

17. Sweating or condensation of moisture on the outside of a pipe is MOST likely to occur on _____ pipe.

    A. live steam   B. compressed air
    C. hot water   D. cold water

18. Extra strong pipe, as compared to standard pipe of the same nominal size, has _____ diameter.

    A. *the same* outside diameter but a smaller inside
    B. *a larger* outside diameter and a smaller inside
    C. *the same* inside diameter but a larger outside
    D. *a larger* inside and outside diameter

19. You observe a plumber use a hammer to strike the hub and spigot ends of each piece of cast iron pipe before installing it in a soil line.
    This practice is

    A. *poor* because it may nick and weaken the pipe
    B. *poor* because it may break the brittle cast iron
    C. *good* because it loosens any rust which may have gathered
    D. *good* because it enables the plumber to tell if the pipe is sound

20. If a drain line pitches one foot in a length of 48 feet, the pitch of the line is MOST NEARLY _____ per foot.

    A. 1/4"   B. 3/8"   C. 1/2"   D. 3/4"

21. A plumbing sketch is drawn to a scale of eighth-size.
    A line measuring 3" on the sketch would be equivalent to _____ feet.

    A. 2   B. 6   C. 12   D. 24

22. Plumbing riser diagrams are GENERALLY drawn to _____ scale.

    A. no
    B. 1/8" = 1'0"
    C. 1/4" = 1'0"
    D. 1/2" = 1'0"

23. A building has a color marked dual water distribution system, one potable water and the other non-potable. The color used to identify the potable water system is

    A. yellow   B. orange   C. green   D. blue

24. Of the following potable water supply systems, the one which is NOT considered to be an auxiliary potable water supply system is a

    A. street main water supply system
    B. elevated gravity water supply system
    C. hydropneumatic pressure booster
    D. water pressure pump system

25. A pit and cover and/or manhole with cover is required for a building (house) trap when the distance from the center-line of the drain to the floor exceeds

    A. 12"   B. 16"   C. 18"   D. 24"

26. The MINIMUM rinse water temperature that can be used in a commercial type dishwasher is _____ °F.

    A. 140   B. 160   C. 180   D. 200

27. Assume that the flow rate through a grease interceptor is 60 g.p.m.
Under this flow rate, the grease interceptor should have a minimum *grease retention capacity* of _____ pounds.

   A. 6　　　B. 30　　　C. 60　　　D. 120

28. The MAIN purpose for increasing the diameter of a vent stack from 2" to 4" when going through a roof is to

   A. provide sufficient area for proper flashing
   B. minimize clogging by hoarfrost
   C. increase the stability of the stack
   D. facilitate testing procedures

29. A pot of wiping solder is overheated.
If this wiping soldier is used, the appearance of the wiped joint would MOST likely be

   A. flaky　　　　　　　　　　B. spotted with bright specks
   C. frosty　　　　　　　　　　D. coarse and grainy

30. Assume that the end of a piece of pipe has been threaded with a well-constructed threading pipe die.
The number of imperfect threads that would be formed due to the chamfer on the die would be MOST NEARLY

   A. zero　　　B. 2 1/2　　　C. 3 1/2　　　D. 4 1/2

31. A pipe threading die with four chasers is used to thread the end of a length of pipe. The resultant threads are rough and torn.
This condition is MOST probably caused by

   A. an improper lip angle
   B. too little clearance between the heel of the chaser and the work
   C. insufficient chip space
   D. not using a cutting oil

32. A deep seal trap has a minimum liquid seal of

   A. 2"　　　B. 3"　　　C. 4"　　　D. 5"

33. Of the following installations, the one which does NOT conform to the plumbing code (i.e., illegal) is the installation of a

   A. water closet with a 4" x 3" closet bend
   B. shower receptor with a 3" drain outlet
   C. washdown urinal with an integral strainer
   D. ball cock in a flush tank 1" above the floor rim of the bowl and provided with a vacuum breaker

34. A *dual vent* is commonly known as a _____ vent.

   A. crown　　　B. common　　　C. side　　　D. yoke

35. Of the following piping materials, the one which is NOT used for potable water service is

   A. copper pipe　　　　　　　B. type *L* tubing
   C. type *K* tubing　　　　　　D. type *TP* tubing

36. The discharge rate for an ejector pump is 100 g.p.m. The *fixture unit value* for this pump is

   A. 10   B. 50   C. 75   D. 100

37. The flood level rim of a fixture is defined as

   A. the invert or bottom of the overflow
   B. the inside top of the overflow pipe
   C. 1" above the top of the overflow pipe
   D. the top edge or rim of the fixture

38. Of the following statements, the one which BEST defines the plumbing term *cross-connection* is the connection between

   A. the domestic hot water and potable cold water
   B. steam and a potable water supply
   C. potable water at 40 psig and potable water at 90 psig
   D. two different potable water distribution pipes

39. Of the following types of water closets, the one which shall be used for public use is the _____ type.

   A. elongated bowl   B. pan
   C. washout   D. offset

40. The MAXIMUM interval between hangers for supporting horizontal 1 1/2" diameter threaded pipe is _____ feet.

   A. 6   B. 8   C. 10   D. 12

KEY (CORRECT ANSWERS)

1.	A	11.	B	21.	A	31.	A
2.	C	12.	C	22.	A	32.	B
3.	D	13.	A	23.	C	33.	C
4.	B	14.	C	24.	A	34.	B
5.	A	15.	B	25.	C	35.	B
6.	C	16.	C	26.	C	36.	D
7.	D	17.	D	27.	D	37.	D
8.	C	18.	A	28.	B	38.	B
9.	A	19.	D	29.	D	39.	A
10.	D	20.	A	30.	C	40.	D

TEST 2

DIRECTIONS: Each question or incomplete statement is followed by several suggested answers or completions. Select the one that BEST answers the question or completes the statement. *PRINT THE LETTER OF THE CORRECT ANSWER IN THE SPACE AT THE RIGHT.*

1. The pipe fitting which should be used to connect a 1" pipe to a 1 1/2" valve is a

    A. reducing elbow
    B. bushing
    C. reducing coupling
    D. street ell

2. A 2 percent pitch in a pipe line is MOST NEARLY equal to a slope of _____ to the foot.

    A. 1/16"   B. 1/8"   C. 1/4"   D. 1/2"

3. The MAIN function of a standpipe system in a building is to

    A. supply water for the roof tank
    B. keep the hot water circulating in order to maintain a constant temperature
    C. provide water for use in case of fire
    D. increase the pressure in the water supply piping

4. The one of the following valves which offers the LEAST resistance to the flow of water is a(n) _____ valve.

    A. check   B. gate   C. globe   D. angle

5. The cast iron drainage fitting that is called a Tucker connection has

    A. male threads on one end and female threads on the other end
    B. one end in the form of a hub and female threads on the other end
    C. one end in the form of a hub and male threads on the other end
    D. each end in the form of a hub

6. When bending copper tubing in the field, special equipment is required _____ -temper tubing.

    A. only for hard
    B. only for soft
    C. for both soft-temper and hard
    D. for neither soft-temper nor hard.

7. If the diameter of the vertical stack in a building is smaller than the diameter of the house drain which connects to it, then the bend which joins them should be

    A. *at least* one size smaller than the stack
    B. *at least* one size larger than the stack
    C. *at least* one size larger than the drain
    D. *larger* than both the stack and the drain

8. If water is flowing into the top of a tank at the rate of 150 gallons per hour and flowing out at the rate of 3/4 of a gallon every 20 seconds, then the amount of water in the tank is _____ gallon per minute.

    A. *increasing* by 1/4
    B. *increasing* by 3/4
    C. *decreasing* by 1/4
    D. *decreasing* by 3/4

9. A flexible coupling between a pump shaft and a motor shaft is GENERALLY provided in order to

   A. reduce the load on the pump
   B. permit excess heat to escape
   C. permit minor misalignment between the shafts
   D. increase the power of the motor

10. The BEST way to prevent a water pocket from forming when two horizontal steam pipes of different diameter are joined is to

    A. use an eccentric fitting
    B. use a long fitting so that the slope between the pipes is very gradual
    C. provide a drain cock
    D. slope the pipe so that the smaller pipe is lower

11. The BEST way to make a temporary repair in a water line with a small leak is by

    A. wrapping a rag around it
    B. welding or brazing
    C. using a clamped patch
    D. drilling, tapping, and inserting a plug

12. Brass is an alloy of

    A. lead and copper
    B. lead and tin
    C. tin and copper
    D. zinc and copper

13. The information that a plumber would NOT normally expect to find on each section of cast iron pipe delivered from the factory is the

    A. manufacturer's name
    B. weight category
    C. diameter
    D. length

14. Steel pipe is GENERALLY connected to copper tubing by

    A. brazing
    B. soldering
    C. wiping
    D. special fittings

15. Pipe is galvanized by coating it with

    A. chrome   B. tin   C. aluminum   D. zinc

16. A return bend in a pipe line changes the direction of flow by

    A. 45°   B. 90°   C. 135°   D. 180°

17. When lagging is used on steam pipes, its MAIN function is to

    A. compensate for expansion
    B. prevent corrosion
    C. reduce radiation heat loss
    D. reduce steam leaks

18. If the drawing of a piping layout is made to a scale of 1/4" equals one foot, then a 7'9" length of piping would be represented by a scaled length on the drawing of APPROXIMATELY _____ inches.

    A. 2   B. 7 3/4   C. 23 1/4   D. 31

19. A pipe reducing coupling normally has _____ thread(s).

    A. two female
    B. two male
    C. one continuous female
    D. one male and one female

20. All bullhead tees have run openings which are

    A. smaller than the outlet
    B. larger than the outlet
    C. of the same size
    D. of different sizes

21. A close nipple

    A. has a short section with no threads
    B. is always less than 3/4" long
    C. has ends of different diameters
    D. has threads over its entire length

22. A reducing tee ALWAYS has

    A. one opening which is larger than the other two
    B. openings of three different sizes
    C. a branch opening which is smaller than the run
    D. a branch which is at an angle of 45 degrees to the run

23. In addition to acting as a filler between threads, pipe joint compound ALSO acts as a

    A. lubricant   B. hardener
    C. coolant   D. permanent bond

24. The valve which is used to permit flow of water in one direction only is called a _____ valve.

    A. check   B. globe   C. gate   D. angle

25. A method which should be used to free a pipe die from chips while threading a pipe is to

    A. use as little lubricating oil as possible
    B. set the die loosely on the pipe stock
    C. clean the chips off the pipe after each thread is cut
    D. partially back off the die at intervals during the turning process

26. The MAIN difference between making up horizontal and vertical caulked joints in cast iron pipe is that, when making up a vertical caulked joint, you should NOT use a

    A. smaller amount of lead
    B. smaller amount of oakum
    C. pouring rope
    D. special caulking tool

27. Assume that a 2" pipe is connected to a 3" pipe by means of a coupling. If the velocity of flow in the 2" pipe is 36 feet per second, then the velocity of flow in the 3" pipe is APPROXIMATELY _____ feet per second.

    A. 16   B. 24   C. 54   D. 81

28. When ordering a cross which is to have two outlet openings which are 1" in diameter and two run openings which are 1 1/2" in diameter, a plumber should specify a _____ cross. 28.____

    A. 1" x 1 1/2" x 1" x 1 1/2"   B. 1 1/2" x 1" x 1 1/2" x 1"
    C. 1" x 1 1/2"   D. 1 1/2" x 1"

29. The LEAST likely cause of a leak in a threaded pipe joint is that 29.____

    A. not enough pipe joint compound was used
    B. the threads are not smooth
    C. the number of threads is not sufficient
    D. too much pipe joint compound has been used

30. The BEST way to assemble a line of piping between a waste stack and a trapped fixture is to 30.____

    A. start at the fixture and work toward the waste stack
    B. start at the waste stack and work toward the fixture
    C. let the order of assembly be determined by the details of the proposed installation
    D. work from the most accessible location

31. When referring to a building drainage system, the term *waste pipe* should NORMALLY be applied to 31.____

    A. piping which does not receive human waste
    B. piping which drains water closets
    C. any pipe which carries water-borne wastes
    D. any pipe which connects to the building drain

32. The one of the following which has the SMALLEST *fixture unit rating* is a 32.____

    A. drinking fountain   B. wash basin
    C. slop sink   D. shower head

33. Pipe joint compound should be applied on 33.____

    A. the threads of male fittings only
    B. the threads of female fittings only
    C. the threads of both male and female fittings
    D. either male or female threads, depending on the type of fitting

34. If a pipe with an outside diameter of 7" is to be fastened against the ceiling with a U-strap, the distance from the ceiling around the pipe and back to the ceiling should be APPROXIMATELY _____ inches. 34.____

    A. 14   B. 16   C. 18   D. 20

35. The MAIN reason cast iron pipe is particularly suitable for underground service is that it 35.____

    A. resists corrosion very well
    B. has a low initial cost
    C. is easy to handle and join
    D. can withstand high pressures

36. The BEST procedure to follow in most cases when a pipe does not screw into a fitting easily is to

    A. use a heavier pipe wrench
    B. cut the threads off the end of the pipe and rethread
    C. attempt to true up defective threads with a die or a tap
    D. heat the fitting with a torch

37. If the hand-operated shut-off valve in a water line is turned to the fully closed position, and water continues to flow through the valve, the MOST likely defect a plumber would expect to find is

    A. a loose gland
    B. excessive packing
    C. improper seating of the valve disc
    D. a loose stuffing nut

38. The MAIN function of a trap in a drainage system is to

    A. prevent freezing of the pipes
    B. block off sewer gases
    C. prevent loss of water pressure
    D. catch rings and other objects

39. A combustible gas which may be present in sewer air and which is explosive in the presence of oxygen is

    A. carbon dioxide   B. freon
    C. hydrogen sulfide   D. nitrogen

40. The MAIN function of a back-pressure valve which is sometimes found in the connection between a water drain pipe and the sewer system is to

    A. equalize the pressure between the drain pipe and the sewer
    B. prevent sewer water from flowing into the drain pipe
    C. provide pressure to enable waste to reach the sewer
    D. make sure that there is not too much water pressure in the sewer line

KEY (CORRECT ANSWERS)

1. B	11. C	21. D	31. A
2. C	12. D	22. C	32. A
3. C	13. D	23. A	33. A
4. B	14. D	24. A	34. C
5. B	15. D	25. D	35. A
6. A	16. D	26. C	36. C
7. B	17. C	27. A	37. C
8. A	18. A	28. D	38. B
9. C	19. A	29. D	39. C
10. A	20. A	30. B	40. B

TEST 3

DIRECTIONS: Each question or incomplete statement is followed by several suggested answers or completions. Select the one that BEST answers the question or completes the statement. *PRINT THE LETTER OF THE CORRECT ANSWER IN THE SPACE AT THE RIGHT.*

1. The piping of a newly installed drainage system shall be tested upon completion of the rough plumbing with a head of water of NOT LESS THAN _____ feet.   1._____

   A. 10   B. 15   C. 20   D. 25

2. The one of the following which should NOT be considered as a *water conserving device* is a(n)   2._____

   A. evaporative condenser B. water cooling tower
   C. spray pond D. water closet

3. In high pressure steam heating systems, the steam pressure is GREATER than _____ psig.   3._____

   A. 15   B. 20   C. 25   D. 30

4. Type *K* water service pipe is made of   4._____

   A. cast iron B. copper
   C. lead D. galvanized steel

5. All water services shall be installed below the finished ground surface at a distance of AT LEAST _____ feet.   5._____

   A. 2   B. 4   C. 6   D. 8

6. The piping in all buildings having dual water distribution systems shall be identified by a color coding of _____ for potable water lines and _____ for non-potable water lines.   6._____

   A. green; red B. green; yellow
   C. yellow; green D. yellow; red

7. In buildings over four stories high, approved plastic pipe may be used for   7._____

   A. water service pipe only
   B. all water distribution system piping
   C. all drainage system piping
   D. chemical waste drainage systems only

8. The minimum required diameter of any soil stack extension which passes through the roof is _____ inches.   8._____

   A. 3   B. 4   C. 5   D. 6

9. A device used to prevent backflow by siphonic action is called a   9._____

   A. relief valve B. sewage ejector
   C. foot valve D. vacuum breaker

10. The MAXIMUM distance permitted between cleanouts in horizontal drainage lines is _____ feet.

    A. 10 B. 30 C. 50 D. 70

11. A horizontal drainage pipe must have a minimum slope of 1/4" per foot if the pipe diameter measures _____ inches.

    A. 2 B. 4 C. 6 D. 8

12. Curb valves should be installed on all domestic service pipes with a diameter larger than _____ inch(es).

    A. 1 B. 1 1/2 C. 2 D. 2 1/2

13. A public water supply system shall be deemed available to a two-family dwelling if a property line of such dwelling is within a distance from the public water supply which is NO GREATER THAN _____ feet.

    A. 50 B. 100 C. 150 D. 200

14. The minimum pressure available near a faucet or water outlet with the water outlet wide open shall be _____ psi.

    A. 2 B. 4 C. 6 D. 8

15. When it is necessary to open a sidewalk in order to do plumbing work, a permit shall be obtained from the department of

    A. water resources
    B. public works
    C. buildings
    D. highways

16. The MINIMUM number of fixture units allowed for a bathroom group containing one lavatory, one bathtub, and one water closet (flush tank) is

    A. 4 B. 6 C. 8 D. 10

17. The MINIMUM number of plumbing fixtures required for a particular type of building occupancy depends MAINLY on

    A. the number of persons expected to use the building
    B. whether the building is publicly or privately owned
    C. the load factor numbers
    D. the age group of the occupants

18. The waste water which would be MOST likely to corrode a cast iron pipe would have a pH value of

    A. 3.0 B. 5.0 C. 7.0 D. 9.0

19. The MAIN factor to consider in determining whether permission from a city department is required before connecting automatic power pumps directly to the street main is the

    A. total water storage capacity in the building
    B. total automatic pump capacity
    C. number of persons expected to occupy the building
    D. number of fixture units in the building

20. In locations where tags are used to designate certain water lines, non-potable water lines should be identified by _____ tags which say _____.

   A. round; WATER UNSAFE
   B. triangular; WATER UNSAFE
   C. round; UNSAFE FOR DRINKING
   D. triangular; UNSAFE FOR DRINKING

21. Trap seals should be vented so that they are at no time subjected to a pressure differential of MORE THAN

   A. 1 inch of water
   B. 2 inches of water
   C. .1 pound per square inch
   D. .2 pound per square inch

22. One trap may serve more than one drain if none of the drains are at a greater distance from the trap than _____ feet.

   A. 5   B. 10   C. 15   D. 20

23. With the exception of commercial dishwashers or laundries, hot water may NOT be discharged into any part of a drainage system at a temperature above

   A. 150°   B. 160°   C. 170°   D. 180°

24. A type of hospital equipment which does NOT require an air gap on the water supply is a(n)

   A. operating table   B. aspirator
   C. toilet   D. sterilizer

25. The percentage of the total connected fixture unit flow rate is likely to occur at any point in the drainage system is called the

   A. discharge coefficient   B. velocity coefficient
   C. load factor   D. hydraulic factor

26. The top edge over which water in a receptacle can overflow is called the

   A. inlet rim   B. air-gap level
   C. drain level   D. flood-level rim

27. A device designed to separate and retain undesirable matter from normal wastes and permit normal sewage to discharge into the disposal terminal is called a(n)

   A. catch basin   B. dead end
   C. seepage pit   D. interceptor

28. Paint is NOT permitted on the jointing material at a joint in cast iron pipe

   A. at any time
   B. until two days after construction of the joint
   C. until the entire plumbing installation is complete
   D. until after the joint has been tested and accepted

29. Wall-hung trough urinals are permitted in

    A. public bath houses
    B. only in temporary locations
    C. where a limited number of people are expected to use them
    D. under no circumstances

30. Drainage pipe cleanouts are required

    A. to be not more than 80 feet apart in a horizontal direction
    B. to extend horizontally from an underground drain
    C. at each change of direction greater than 45°
    D. to be 3/4 of the nominal size of pipe for diameters up to 4 inches

31. All water used in the construction of a building shall be metered if the building is higher than _____ stories.

    A. 3   B. 4   C. 5   D. 6

32. Gas piping should be tested under a pressure of NO LESS THAN _____ psig.

    A. 3   B. 5   C. 7   D. 9

33. When installing gas lines in a building, it is permissible to

    A. reuse gas pipe which has been removed from an existing installation
    B. use gas piping for an electrical ground
    C. use malleable iron fittings
    D. use gasket unions.

34. If the water pressure in the street main is 100 psi,

    A. a gravity tank shall be installed on the roof
    B. the pressure at the closed fixtures shall be reduced to 85 psi
    C. a stop-and-waste valve shall be installed underground
    D. a booster pump shall be connected to the main

35. When modernizing a multiple dwelling, a plumbing permit is required if

    A. several broken toilets are to be replaced by new fixtures
    B. an additional washing machine and standpipe are to be installed in the laundry room
    C. gas stoves in all apartments are to be replaced by a newer model
    D. the hot water storage tank is to be replaced

36. When an adjoining building is erected next to an existing building which is higher, all waste stacks of the new building shall be located a distance from the common lot line of AT LEAST _____ feet.

    A. 5   B. 10   C. 15   D. 20

37. A type of trap which is prohibited is the _____ trap.

    A. S   B. 1/2S   C. bottle   D. running

38. Air chambers installed at individual fixtures 38.____

    A. need not be accessible
    B. shall be accessible
    C. are required for loads of less than 5 fixture units
    D. are required for loads of more than 5 fixture units

39. In the installation of a hot water storage tank, it is PROHIBITED to install a 39.____

    A. combination pressure and temperature relief valve
    B. separate pressure relief valve and separate temperature relief valve
    C. pressure relief valve whose opening pressure is greater than 25 lbs. above normal system working pressure
    D. check valve between the relief valve and the storage tank

40. Sanitary drainage piping must be sloped so that the minimum velocity of flow is _____ ft. per second. 40.____

KEY (CORRECT ANSWERS)

1. A	11. A	21. A	31. D
2. D	12. C	22. C	32. A
3. A	13. B	23. A	33. C
4. B	14. D	24. C	34. B
5. B	15. D	25. C	35. B
6. B	16. B	26. D	36. B
7. D	17. A	27. D	37. C
8. B	18. A	28. D	38. A
9. D	19. B	29. B	39. D
10. C	20. B	30. C	40. C

EXAMINATION SECTION
TEST 1

DIRECTIONS: Each question or incomplete statement is followed by several suggested answers or completions. Select the one that BEST answers the question or completes the statement. *PRINT THE LETTER OF THE CORRECT ANSWER IN THE SPACE AT THE RIGHT.*

1. A fitting with a 1/8th bend would be used to make an offset of about _____ degrees. 1._____

    A. 11 1/4 B. 22 1/2 C. 45 D. 67 1/2

2. To dig a trench 3'0" wide, 50'0" long, and 5'6" deep, the total number of cubic yards of earth to be removed is MOST NEARLY 2._____

    A. 30 B. 90 C. 140 D. 825

3. The percentage of copper in *Red Brass Pipe* which conforms to standard specifications is about 3._____

    A. 25 B. 50 C. 60 D. 85

4. A fixture unit is equal to a water discharge rate of one 4._____

    A. cubic foot per minute
    B. cubic foot per second
    C. gallon per minute
    D. gallon per second

5. The total length of four pieces of 2" pipe, whose lengths are 7'3 1/2", 4'2 3/16", 5'7 5/16", and 8'5 7/8", respectively, is 5._____

    A. 24'6 3/4"
    B. 24'7 15/16"
    C. 25'5 13/16"
    D. 25'6 7/8"

6. Under the same conditions, the group of pipes that gives the same flow as one 6" pipe is (neglecting friction) _____ pipes. 6._____

    A. 3 3" B. 4 3" C. 2 4" D. 3 4"

7. The PRIMARY difference between a schedule 40 pipe and a schedule 80 pipe, of the same material and size, is that schedule 80 pipe 7._____

    A. weighs more per foot
    B. has fewer threads per inch
    C. has a larger inside diameter
    D. has a thinner wall thickness

8. The purpose of a vacuum breaker used with an automatic flush valve is to 8._____

    A. limit the flow of water to the fixture
    B. control the water pressure to the fixture
    C. equalize the water pressure
    D. prevent pollution of the water supply

9. Wiping solder for lead pipe usually has a melting range of _____ to _____ °F. 9._____

    A. 150; 250 B. 251; 350 C. 360; 470 D. 475; 60

10. The fixture with the LARGEST fixture unit rating would be a 10.____

   A. water closet B. urinal
   C. slop sink D. lavatory

11. Vents to the outer air are required to be installed at plumbing fixtures for the purpose of 11.____

   A. removing room odors
   B. preventing the sewer from backing up into the fixtures
   C. preventing the siphoning of traps
   D. obtaining rapid removal of wastes

12. Where it is required to keep friction resistance to a minimum in a piping layout, the type 12.____
    of valve to be used is a _____ valve.

   A. gate B. globe C. angle D. needle

13. A CORRECT statement is that the number of threads cut per inch on standard pipe 13.____

   A. *increases* as the diameter of pipe increases
   B. *decreases* as the diameter of pipe increases
   C. *remains constant* for all diameters of pipe
   D. *depends* on the length of thread to be cut on the pipe

14. The plan for a plumbing installation which is to be renovated by your crew shows the use 14.____
    of certain types of fittings which you believe to be wrong.
    Your PROPER procedure would be to

   A. immediately report the error to your superior
   B. use the fittings according to the plan
   C. hold up the job until you have checked with the man who delivered the material
   D. use the type of fitting you believe to be correct and revise the plan

15. A water pipe is to run under a structural beam and be suspended from the beam. 15.____
    The pipe should be suspended by a hanger _____ the beam.

   A. passing through a hole in the web of
   B. passing through a hole in the flange of
   C. welded to
   D. clamped to

16. It is INCORRECT to say that 16.____

   A. a gasoline torch must be fully filled with gasoline
   B. there is a difference between fittings for threaded drainage pipe and fittings for ordinary threaded pipe
   C. for pipe designated as 200 WOG, the letters stand for water, oil, gas
   D. loose parts in a faucet may cause noisy operation

17. If the drain of a sink frequently emits a gurgling sound, it is MOST probable that the 17.____

   A. drain plug of the sink trap leaks
   B. sink trap is partially blocked by some solids
   C. drain line is pitched in the wrong direction
   D. venting for the sink trap is imperfect

18. If a set of plumbing plans are drawn to a scale of 1 1/2" to the foot, the plans are said to be one _____ size. 18.____

    A. half
    B. quarter
    C. eighth
    D. sixteenth

19. The length of 3/4" pipe which should be allowed for screwing into a 3/4" elbow when laying out a job is MOST NEARLY 19.____

    A. 1"   B. 7/8"   C. 1/2"   D. 1/4"

20. The type of valve which is generally used for controlling the water flow in a plumbing system is a 20.____

    A. gate valve
    B. globe valve
    C. needle valve
    D. plug cock

KEY (CORRECT ANSWERS)

1.	C	11.	C
2.	A	12.	A
3.	D	13.	B
4.	A	14.	A
5.	D	15.	D
6.	B	16.	A
7.	A	17.	B
8.	D	18.	C
9.	C	19.	C
10.	A	20.	B

TEST 2

DIRECTIONS: Each question or incomplete statement is followed by several suggested answers or completions. Select the one that BEST answers the question or completes the statement. *PRINT THE LETTER OF THE CORRECT ANSWER IN THE SPACE AT THE RIGHT.*

Questions 1-6.

DIRECTIONS: Questions 1 through 6, inclusive, are to be answered in accordance with plumbing code requirements.

1. The MINIMUM distance that a vacuum breaker must be set above the flood level rim of a fixture is

    A. 2" B. 4" C. 6" D. 8"

2. The MINIMUM weight of a 5-foot length of a 4-inch single hub *extra heavy* cast iron soil pipe should be, in pounds,

    A. 40 B. 50 C. 60 D. 70

3. Horizontal drainage piping shall be run in practical alignment and at uniform grade per foot of AT LEAST

    A. 1/8" B. 1/4" C. 1/2" D. 1"

4. A pressure relief valve shall be provided in a hot water supply system and, between this relief valve and the water heating boiler, there shall be installed _____ valve.

    A. a gate
    C. a globe
    B. a check
    D. no other

5. When soil waste and vent pipes are extended through a roof, they must have a diameter of AT LEAST

    A. 3" B. 4" C. 5" D. 6"

6. The type of pipe NOT permitted for underground use is that made of

    A. cast iron
    C. brass
    B. lead
    D. galvanized steel

7. The MAXIMUM theoretical suction lift of water pumps, expressed in feet of water at sea level elevation, is MOST NEARLY _____ feet.

    A. 36 B. 32 C. 28 D. 24

8. The type of pipe that should NOT be used for drainage within a building is

    A. vitrified clay
    C. bronze
    B. cast iron
    D. copper

9. A 5" drain 25' long is to be installed with a pitch of 1/4" per foot, the difference in elevation of the two ends of the drain is

    A. 1 1/4" B. 5" C. 6 1/4" D. 7 1/4"

10. When threading pipe with properly adjusted and correctly made pipe dies, the PROPER thread is obtained when

    A. three threads protrude the die
    B. five non-taper threads are made
    C. the pipe end is flush with the face of the dies
    D. the thread length is approximately twice the diameter of the pipe

11. A hot water line made of copper has a straight horizontal run of 150 feet and when installed is at a temperature of 45° F. In use its temperature rises to 190° F.
    If the coefficient of expansion for copper is 0.0000095" per foot per degree F., the total expansion, in inches, in the run of pipe is given by the product of 150 multiplied by 0.0000095 by

    A. 145
    B. 145 x 12
    C. 145 divided by 12
    D. 145 x 12 x 12

12. The use of hard water in piping systems is *undesirable* MAINLY because it causes

    A. leaky joints
    B. corrosion
    C. high friction losses
    D. scaling

13. A water storage tank measures 5' long, 4' wide, and 6' deep and is filled to the 5 1/2' mark with water.
    If one cubic foot of water weighs 62 pounds, the number of pounds of water required to COMPLETELY fill the tank is

    A. 7440   B. 6200   C. 1240   D. 620

14. The BASIC function of a trap on a drainage system is to prevent

    A. sewer gases from entering the house
    B. waterborne diseases
    C. blocking the drainage
    D. insects from entering the house through the drain pipe

15. The INCORRECTLY matched pair is

    A. wiped joint - lead pipe
    B. swedge and solder joint - copper pipe
    C. caulked joint - wiped joint
    D. screw thread joint - wrought pipe

16. For BEST results, the coil of an indirect water heater should be connected so that the top of the coil is connected to the _____ of the tank.

    A. lower opening on the side
    B. opening in the bottom
    C. hot water outlet on top
    D. top opening in the side

17. The one fitting NOT used in a plumbing installation is

    A. street ell
    B. Y branch
    C. angle folds
    D. reducing tee

18. The CORRECTLY matched pair is:

    A. Hot water heating system - quick vent air valve
    B. Hot radiators - convection air currents
    C. Expansion tank - steam-heating system
    D. Altitude gauge - steam-heating system

19. A pipe reamer is used to

    A. thread pipe
    B. enlarge the size of a pipe
    C. remove burrs from the inside of a pipe
    D. join pipes of different sizes

20. A 5-inch length of pipe with male threads at each end is called a

    A. stud   B. coupling   C. sleeve   D. nipple

18.___

19.___

20.___

KEY (CORRECT ANSWERS)

1.	B	11.	A
2.	C	12.	D
3.	A	13.	D
4.	D	14.	A
5.	B	15.	C
6.	D	16.	D
7.	B	17.	C
8.	A	18.	B
9.	C	19.	C
10.	C	20.	D

EXAMINATION SECTION
TEST 1

DIRECTIONS: Each question or incomplete statement is followed by several suggested answers or completions. Select the one that BEST answers the question or completes the statement. *PRINT THE LETTER OF THE CORRECT ANSWER IN THE SPACE AT THE RIGHT.*

Questions 1-5.

DIRECTIONS: Questions 1 through 5, inclusive, are to be answered by referring to the following symbols that would be used on a piping drawing for pipe fittings and valves.

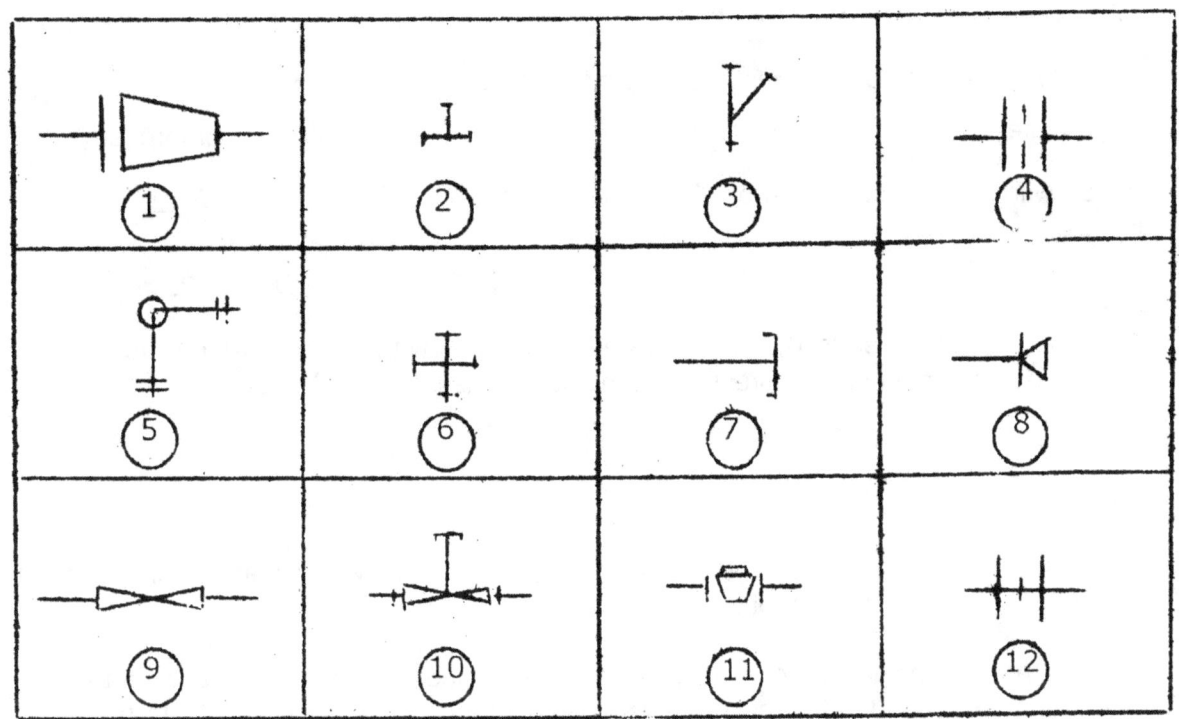

1. The symbol representing a pipe plug is numbered
   A. 1 B. 8 C. 9 D. 11

2. The symbol representing a screwed gate valve is numbered
   A. 5 B. 7 C. 9 D. 12

3. The symbol representing a union is numbered
   A. 3 B. 4 C. 8 D. 12

4. The symbol representing a reducing flange is numbered
   A. 1 B. 2 C. 5 D. 9

5. The symbol representing a screwed lateral is numbered
   A. 1 B. 3 C. 5 D. 7

1.____
2.____
3.____
4.____
5.____

6. A piping sketch is drawn to a scale of 1/8" = 1 foot. A vertical steam line measuring 3 1/2" on the sketch would have an ACTUAL length of _____ feet.

   A. 16   B. 22   C. 24   D. 28

7. Three lengths of pipe 1'10", 3'2 1/2", and 5'7 1/2", respectively, are to be cut from a pipe 14'0" long. Allowing 1/8" for each pipe cut, the length of pipe remaining is

   A. 3'1 1/8"   B. 3'2 1/2"   C. 3'3 1/4"   D. 3'3 5/8"

8. According to the building code, the MAXIMUM permitted surface temperature of combustible construction materials located near heating equipment is

   A. 170° F   B. 195° F   C. 210° F   D. 220° F

9. A condensate pump discharges hot condensate to a

   A. boiler   B. sewer   C. well   D. compressor

10. A pipe with an outside diamter of 4" has a circumference of MOST NEARLY _____ inches.

    A. 8.05   B. 9.81   C. 12.57   D. 14.92

11. A steam gauge that reads 120 psi is located 20 feet below the point at which it is connected to a steam main. The pressure in the steam main is MOST NEARLY _____ psi.

    A. 111   B. 100   C. 80   D. 67

Questions 12-16.

DIRECTIONS: Questions 12 through 16, inclusive, are to be answered in accordance with the following paragraph.

The thickness of insulation necessary for the most economical results varies with the steam temperature. The standard covering consists of 85 percent magnesia with 10 percent of long-fibre asbestos as a binder. Both magnesia and laminated asbestos - felt and other forms of mineral wool including glass wool - are also used for heat insulation. The magnesia and laminated asbestos coverings may be safely used at temperatures up to 600° F. Pipe insulation is applied in molded sections 3 feet long. The sections are attached to the pipe by means of galvanized iron wire or netting. Flanges and fittings can be insulated by direct application of magnesia cement to the metal without *reinforcement*. Insulation should always be maintained in good condition because it saves fuel. Routine maintenance of warm-pipe insulation should include prompt repair of damaged surfaces. Steam and hot water leaks concealed by insulation will be difficult to detect. Underground steam or hot-water pipes are best insulated using a concrete trench with removable cover.

12. The word *reinforcement*, as used above, means MOST NEARLY

    A. resistance   B. strengthening
    C. regulation   D. removal

13. According to the above paragraph, magnesia and laminated asbestos coverings may be safely used at temperatures up to

    A. 800° F   B. 720° F   C. 675° F   D. 600° F

14. According to the above paragraph, insulation should ALWAYS be maintained in good condition because it   14.____

    A. is laminated
    B. saves fuel
    C. is attached to the pipe
    D. prevents leaks

15. According to the above paragraph, pipe insulation sections are attached to the pipe by means of   15.____

    A. binders
    B. mineral wool
    C. netting
    D. staples

16. According to the above paragraph, a leak in a hot-water pipe may be difficult to detect because, when insulation is used, the leak is   16.____

    A. underground
    B. hidden
    C. routine
    D. cemented

17. The power source of a pneumatic tool is   17.____

    A. manual
    B. water pressure
    C. compressed air
    D. electricity

18. The tool used to cut internal pipe threads is a   18.____

    A. broach
    B. tap
    C. die
    D. rod

19. Of the following tools, the one that should be used to cut thin-wall metal tubing is the   19.____

    A. reamer
    B. plier
    C. hacksaw
    D. broach

20. A wrench that can be used to tighten a nut to a specified tightness is a _____ wrench.   20.____

    A. bonney
    B. spud
    C. torque
    D. adjustable

KEY (CORRECT ANSWERS)

1.	B	11.	A
2.	C	12.	B
3.	D	13.	D
4.	A	14.	B
5.	B	15.	C
6.	D	16.	B
7.	D	17.	C
8.	A	18.	B
9.	A	19.	C
10.	C	20.	C

TEST 2

DIRECTIONS: Each question or incomplete statement is followed by several suggested answers or completions. Select the one that BEST answers the question or completes the statement. *PRINT THE LETTER OF THE CORRECT ANSWER IN THE SPACE AT THE RIGHT.*

1. The one of the following that will MOST likely show a *mushroomed* head is a

    A. cold chisel
    B. file cleaner
    C. screwdriver blade
    D. ratchet

2. A tool that is used to bend pipe is the

    A. lintel B. hickey C. collet D. brace

3. Of the following types of fire extinguishers, the one that should be used to extinguish an electrical fire is the _____ fire extinguisher.

    A. soda acid
    B. foam
    C. carbon dioxide
    D. water

4. The MAIN reason for grounding electrical equipment is to

    A. increase power to the coils
    B. increase wattage in the line
    C. prevent serious short circuits
    D. protect personnel from electrical shock

5. When disconnecting the electric wires from a motor, it is GOOD practice to

    A. cut the live power wires
    B. assume that the circuit is alive
    C. scrape the terminals
    D. nick the wire in several places first

6. A SAFE procedure to follow when using a straight-type ladder is to

    A. use a box or stair to support the ladder legs
    B. hang tools on the ladder so they cannot be dropped
    C. take one step at a time when climbing
    D. have an assistant climb behind you to protect you

7. Safety in work habits is MOST closely related to which of the following?

    A. Worker's knowledge of the job
    B. Speed with which a worker does the job
    C. Wages paid to a worker
    D. Carefulness of a worker

8. When a helper drops oil onto a plant floor, he should

    A. find out who is supposed to clean it up
    B. inform the foreman
    C. dry it up himself
    D. let it soak into the floor

9. Assume that a helper earns $5.58 an hour and that he works 250 seven-hour days a year. His gross yearly salary will be

   A. $9,715   B. $9,765   C. $9,825   D. $9,890

10. A pipe having an inside diameter of 3.48 inches and a wall thickness of .18 inches will have an outside diameter of _____ inches.

    A. 3.84   B. 3.64   C. 3.57   D. 3.51

11. A rectangular steel bar having a volume of 30 cubic inches, a width of 2 inches, and a height of 3 inches will have a length of _____ inches.

    A. 12   B. 10   C. 8   D. 5

12. A pipe weighs 20.4 pounds per foot of length. The TOTAL weight of eight pieces of this pipe with each piece 20 feet in length is MOST NEARLY _____ pounds.

    A. 460   B. 1,680   C. 2,420   D. 3,260

13. According to the building code, all portions of standpipe systems should be painted

    A. black   B. red   C. blue   D. yellow

14. According to the building code, a material acceptable for the fittings of a fire standpipe system above ground is

    A. copper   B. chromium
    C. malleable brass   D. cast steel

15. According to the building code, an uninsulated steam pipe must be a MINIMUM clear distance from combustible materials of _____ inch.

    A. 1/2   B. 1/4   C. 1/8   D. 1/16

Questions 16-20.

DIRECTIONS: Questions 16 through 20, inclusive, are to be answered in accordance with the following paragraph.

Reductions in pipe size of a building heating system are made with eccentric fittings and are pitched downward. The ends of mains with gravity return shall be at least 18" above the water line of the boiler. As condensate flows opposite to the steam runouts are one size larger than the vertical pipe and are pitched upward. In a one-pipe system, an automatic air vent must be provided at each main to relieve air pressure and to let steam enter the radiator. As steam enters the radiator, a *thermal* device causes the vent to close, thereby holding the steam. Steam mains should not be less than two inches in diameter. The end of the steam main should have a minimum size of one-half of its greatest diameter. Small steam systems should be sized for a 2 oz. pressure drop. Large steam systems should be sized for a 4 oz. pressure drop.

16. The word *thermal,* as used in the above paragraph, means MOST NEARLY

    A. convector   B. heat   C. instrument   D. current

17. According to the above paragraph, the one of the following that is one size larger than the vertical pipe is the

    A. steam main
    B. valve
    C. water line
    D. runout

18. According to the above paragraph, small steam systems should be sized for a pressure drop of _____ oz.

    A. 2   B. 3   C. 4   D. 5

19. According to the above paragraph, ends of mains with gravity return shall be AT LEAST

    A. 18" above the water line of the boiler
    B. one-quarter of the greatest diameter of the main
    C. twice the size of the vertical pipe in the main
    D. 18" above the steam line of the boiler

20. According to the above paragraph, the one of the following that is provided at each main to relieve air pressure is a(n)

    A. gravity return
    B. convector
    C. eccentric
    D. vent

KEY (CORRECT ANSWERS)

1.	A	11.	D
2.	B	12.	D
3.	C	13.	B
4.	D	14.	D
5.	B	15.	A
6.	C	16.	B
7.	D	17.	D
8.	C	18.	A
9.	B	19.	A
10.	A	20.	D

EXAMINATION SECTION
TEST 1

DIRECTIONS: Each question or incomplete statement is followed by several suggested answers or completions. Select the one that BEST answers the question or completes the statement. *PRINT THE LETTER OF THE CORRECT ANSWER IN THE SPACE AT THE RIGHT.*

1. To prevent asphalt from sticking to the inner surfaces of a dump truck, the surfaces should be sprayed with

    A. gasoline
    B. water
    C. kerosene
    D. heavy fuel oil

2. A pneumatic roller

    A. is steam powered
    B. has rubber tires
    C. has steel rolls
    D. is diesel powered

3. A trench is 4'0" wide by 8'6" deep by 48'0" long. The volume of earth removed to form this trench, in cubic yards, is MOST NEARLY

    A. 62   B. 60   C. 58   D. 56

4. The presence of lumps in a sheet asphalt mixture is MOST likely an indication that the mixture

    A. is too cold
    B. is too hot
    C. does not contain enough asphaltic cement
    D. contains too much sand

5. The bedding material for granite block pavement is usually

    A. asphalt
    B. concrete
    C. sand
    D. mineral dust

6. Cold patch asphalt is usually shipped by the manufacturer in

    A. steel drums
    B. wooden kegs
    C. cloth sacks
    D. aluminum sacks

7. The proper drainage of a street is LEAST dependent upon the _____ the street.

    A. crown of
    B. gutters of
    C. manholes in
    D. inlets of

8. The dead end of a vitrified pipe sewer should

    A. be closed with a bulkhead of brick masonry
    B. be closed with a wooden bulkhead
    C. have a cast iron gate valve
    D. be left open

9. The ONLY portions of vitrified pipe which should be left partly unglazed or scored with parallel lines are the _____ spigot.

A. *outside* of the hub and the inside of the
B. *inside* of the hub and the outside of the
C. *outside* of both hub and
D. *inside* of both hub and

10. A manhole cover which had few or no openings would MOST likely be used on a manhole built

    A. for a sanitary sewer
    B. for a combined sewer
    C. for a storm sewer
    D. under a sidewalk

11. Bituminous material is normally used to make joints in sewer pipe when the sewer is a _____ sewer _____ the normal water table.

    A. sanitary; above
    B. sanitary; alongside
    C. storm; above
    D. storm; below

12. Assume that Class A concrete is a 1:2:4 mix with 6 gallons of water per sack of cement, and Class B concrete is a 1:2 1/2:5 mix with 6 gallons of water per sack of cement. With reference to the foregoing, the statement MOST NEARLY correct is that the

    A. Class A concrete is much stronger
    B. Class B concrete is much stronger
    C. number of cubic feet of concrete per sack of cement is greater for the Class A concrete
    D. number of cubic feet of concrete per sack of cement is greater for the Class B concrete

13. When fresh concrete is to be placed on concrete that has already set, the one of the following procedures which would be MOST accurate is that the existing surface of concrete should be

    A. cleaned
    B. cleaned and wet down
    C. cleaned, wet down, and roughened
    D. cleaned, wet down, roughened, and coated with a grout of neat cement

14. Assume that a specification reads: Bats may be used in inside ring of arch and inverts for closers only.
    The bats referred to are usually made of

    A. concrete   B. wood   C. brick   D. metal

15. Other things being equal, close sheeting is MOST likely to be required in trenches which are

    A. shallow   B. deep   C. wide   D. narrow

16. Assume that a foreman on a trenching job insists that the road surface adjacent to the trench be swept periodically.
    It is MOST likely that his reason for doing so is PRIMARILY based on consideration of

    A. appearance
    B. safety
    C. fussiness
    D. keeping someone busy

17. The head of a bar that was used to break concrete has been redressed and tempered. 17.____
    This is usually

    A. *good* practice, because a mushroomed head is dangerous
    B. *bad* practice, because it should not have been tempered
    C. *good* practice, because it restores the bar to its original condition
    D. *bad* practice, because it adds to the cost of the job

18. When lifting a heavy object, a man should NOT 18.____

    A. keep his back straight and vertical
    B. place his feet wide apart
    C. bend at the knees to grasp the object
    D. get a firm hold on the object

19. Ignoring the overlap, the length, in inches, of the gasket for a gasket and mortar joint on 19.____
    a 12-inch (internal diameter) pipe with a wall thickness of 1 inch is MOST NEARLY

    A. 38   B. 41   C. 44   D. 47

20. The mortar that is used for a gasket and mortar joint on a vitrified pipe sewer is 20.____

    A. neat cement grout
    B. 1 part cement, 1 to 1 1/2 parts sand, mixed with water
    C. 1 part cement, 3 parts sand, mixed with water
    D. 1 part cement, 1 part sand, 1 part gravel, mixed with water

21. The MOST important function performed by the gasket in a gasket and mortar joint is to 21.____

    A. keep the mortar out of the pipe
    B. reduce the quantity of mortar used
    C. keep the spigot centered in the hub
    D. provide a cushion when the mortar is being rammed

22. The length of a single section of sewer rod that is used for cleaning is usually limited by 22.____

    A. weight considerations
    B. the strength of the material used for the rod
    C. the size of manhole cover
    D. the diameter of manhole at sewer elevation

23. Aside from safety considerations, the MOST important function of close sheeting in 23.____
    trenching is to

    A. prevent undermining of adjacent pavement
    B. improve the appearance of the job
    C. make it easier to use excavating machinery
    D. keep out water

24. Assume that a pump is being used to pump out a deep cellar which has been flooded. 24.____
    Of the following distances, the one which will MOST likely prevent the operation of the
    pump if the distance is too large is the

A. vertical distance between pump and inlet
B. horizontal distance between pump and inlet
C. sloping distance between pump and inlet
D. horizontal distance from pump to outlet

25. A change in the slope of a vitrified pipe sewer should be located 25.____

    A. a few feet upstream from a manhole
    B. a few feet downstream from a manhole
    C. midway between manholes
    D. at a manhole

KEY (CORRECT ANSWERS)

1.	C	11.	A
2.	B	12.	D
3.	B	13.	D
4.	A	14.	C
5.	C	15.	B
6.	A	16.	B
7.	C	17.	B
8.	A	18.	B
9.	B	19.	C
10.	D	20.	B

21.	C
22.	D
23.	A
24.	A
25.	D

TEST 2

DIRECTIONS: Each question or incomplete statement is followed by several suggested answers or completions. Select the one that BEST answers the question or completes the statement. *PRINT THE LETTER OF THE CORRECT ANSWER IN THE SPACE AT THE RIGHT.*

1. Box sheeting differs from regular sheeting PRIMARILY in 1.____

    A. size of timber used for sheeting
    B. that it is used in trenches of short length
    C. that it is used in trenches of greater width
    D. the direction in which the sheeting is placed

2. Assume that sewage is flowing out of three adjacent manholes on a sewer line. It is MOST logical to expect that there is an obstruction 2.____

    A. between the center manhole and the higher one
    B. between the center manhole and the lower one
    C. anywhere between the three manholes
    D. outside the stretch of sewer between the three manholes

3. Earth used to backfill a vitrified pipe sewer trench 3.____

    A. should not contain any stones
    B. may contain stones if the stones are less than 10 inches in largest dimension
    C. should contain only those stones removed from the trench
    D. may contain stones up to 10 inches in largest dimension provided there are no stones in the backfill which is within 2 feet of the pipe

4. When laying bell and spigot sewer pipe, it is GOOD practice to place the ball end 4.____

    A. away from the outlet
    B. toward the outlet
    C. either way
    D. away from the outlet when the sewer has a flat slope

5. The number of board feet in 22 pieces of 2 x 6's, 12'6" long is MOST NEARLY 5.____

    A. 275   B. 270   C. 265   D. 260

6. A riser would MOST likely be used on a _____ sewer. 6.____

    A. shallow   B. vitrified pipe
    C. deep   D. reinforced concrete pipe

7. If, after ramming, a granite block is found to be too low, it should be 7.____

    A. replaced with a thicker block
    B. removed with a pinch bar
    C. covered with mortar
    D. removed with tongs

8. A separating agent, such as calcium chloride, would MOST likely be used on a(n) _____ pavement with _____ filler. 8.____

A. granite block; cement grout
B. asphalt block; cement grout joint
C. granite block; asphaltic joint
D. poured concrete; cement grout joint

9. Assume that granite block has been redressed.
The dimension which is MOST likely to be the same as that on the original block is

   A. length   B. width   C. depth   D. none

10. Spacing strips are MOST likely to be used when laying _____ block pavement with _____ joint filler.

    A. asphalt; cement grout   B. asphalt; asphaltic
    C. granite; cement grout   D. granite; asphaltic

11. The piece of equipment MOST likely to be used both for sheet asphalt pavement and asphalt block pavement is a(n)

    A. tamper   B. smoothing iron
    C. asphalt rake   D. asphalt kettle

12. In cleaning a steel reinforcing bar for reinforced concrete, it is LEAST important to remove

    A. rust   B. grease   C. oil   D. paint

13. Concrete that is used for a concrete base for pavement should have a slump of MOST NEARLY _____ inches.

    A. 10   B. 8   C. 6   D. 3

14. A concrete mix can be made more workable without reducing its strength by adding to the mix

    A. cement   B. water
    C. cement and water D. coarse aggregate

15. Forms for concrete are usually oiled to

    A. prevent honeycombing
    B. make the form watertight
    C. prevent segregation
    D. make stripping easier

16. The backlash in a roller used on sheet asphalt is

    A. *good,* because it makes for faster operation
    B. *good,* because it makes the operator's job easier
    C. *bad,* because it results in waves in the asphalt
    D. *bad,* because it requires more asphaltic cement

17. The LARGEST particles in the binder course of a sheet asphalt pavement usually consists of

    A. broken stone   B. sand
    C. smooth round pebbles   D. rock dust

18. It is important to remove water which has seeped into bell holes in a sewer trench because 18.____

    A. this makes the caulker more comfortable
    B. this water will spoil the joint
    C. this water will preserve the stability of the trench bottom
    D. the water is unsanitary

19. Of the following materials, the one which would be MOST combustible is _____ asphalt. 19.____

    A. RG cutback   B. MC cutback
    C. SC cutback   D. emulsified

20. The one and one-half inch stones of a base for an asphalt macadam pavement have been rolled. 20.____
    The BEST time to apply the asphalt cement is

    A. immediately after the rolling
    B. after the rolled stones have been wet down with water
    C. after sand has been spread over the broken stone
    D. after sand has been spread and rolled

21. The binder course of a sheet asphalt pavement has been laid today. The surface course should be placed 21.____

    A. today   B. tomorrow
    C. the day after tomorrow D. any day next week

Questions 22-23.

DIRECTIONS: Questions 22 and 23 refer to a 12-inch sewer line which is being constructed without a cradle in a clay soil.

22. Before the pipe is placed in the trench, the bottom of the trench should be excavated to a depth of MOST NEARLY _____ inches _____ the invert. 22.____

    A. 12; below   B. 6; below
    C. 12; above   D. 6; above

23. After the pipe is properly bedded, the excavated material should be replaced in layers 23.____

    A. 6 inches thick, each layer being flooded with water
    B. 6 inches thick, each layer being tamped
    C. 4 feet thick, each layer being tamped
    D. 2 feet thick, each layer being flooded with water

24. In sewer work, pargeting would MOST likely be required on 24.____

    A. vitrified pipe sewers
    B. manholes
    C. cast iron pipe sewers
    D. reinforced concrete pipe sewers

25. A seal coat for an asphalt macadam base course has been applied by a pressure distributor.
    Before a seal coat is rolled, it should be

    A. allowed to cool
    B. covered with broken stone
    C. wet down with water
    D. squeegeed over the surface

25. _____

KEY (CORRECT ANSWERS)

1. D
2. D
3. D
4. A
5. A

6. C
7. D
8. C
9. C
10. A

11. D
12. A
13. D
14. C
15. D

16. C
17. A
18. B
19. A
20. A

21. A
22. B
23. B
24. B
25. B

EXAMINATION SECTION
TEST 1

DIRECTIONS: Each question or incomplete statement is followed by several suggested answers or completions. Select the one that BEST answers the question or completes the statement. *PRINT THE LETTER OF THE CORRECT ANSWER IN THE SPACE AT THE RIGHT.*

1. If cast iron weighs 450 pounds per cubic foot, the weight of a solid cast iron manhole cover 2 feet in diameter and 1 inch thick is MOST NEARLY _____ pounds. 1.____
   A. 94 B. 118 C. 136 D. 164

2. A gas which has an odor similar to rotten eggs is 2.____
   A. argon
   C. nitrogen
   B. phosgene
   D. hydrogen sulfide

3. The gases released by digesting sewage sludges contain about 72% 3.____
   A. methane B. chlorine C. helium D. copper

4. In sewer maintenance, an orange peel bucket is USUALLY used for 4.____
   A. testing for toxic gases
   C. cleaning roof drains
   B. rodding sewers
   D. cleaning catch basins

5. A plumbing device that prevents the passage of bad odors and gases from the sewer system to a building is a 5.____
   A. corporation stop
   C. curb box
   B. union
   D. trap

6. An 8-inch diameter sewer enters at the upstream side of a manhole, and a 10-inch sewer leaves at the downstream side. The crowns of the sewers are at the same elevation. If the invert elevation of the 8-inch sewer is 100.64 feet, the invert elevation of the 10-inch sewer is MOST NEARLY _____ feet. 6.____
   A. 100.32 B. 100.41 C. 100.47 D. 100.52

7. Where ground slopes are unfavorable, it is necessary to keep sanitary sewer grades at the minimum velocity that will prevent the settling of material when the sewer is flowing full.
   The velocity is MOST NEARLY _____ feet per second. 7.____
   A. 0.2 B. 2.0 C. 20.0 D. 200.0

8. A condition that will permit polluted water to enter a potable water supply is a 8.____
   A. tide gate
   C. cathodic protection
   B. cross connection
   D. reducer

9. A wheel with a grooved rim such as is mounted in a pulley block to guide rope or cable is a 9.____
   A. turnbuckle
   C. slant
   B. wormgear
   D. sheave

10. A device used in a combined sewer to bypass excess storm-flow is a(n)

    A. soffit
    B. side-flow weir
    C. aquafer
    D. cellular cofferdam

11. A device installed at the discharge end of a sewer outfall which operates to permit gravity flow at low stages in the receiving waters, but closes to prevent backflow when the elevation of the receiving waters is high is a

    A. flume
    B. buttress
    C. tide gate
    D. flocculator

12. A pipe used to carry streamflow under a highway embankment is a

    A. culvert   B. lock   C. standpipe   D. pitot

13. The pipe on the discharge side of a sewage pump is a

    A. tell-tale pipe
    B. sump pipe
    C. suction pipe
    D. force main

14. A model 6520 sewer cleaner is rated at 60 GPM at 1000 PSI. As used here, PSI is an abbreviation for

    A. positive surging inflow
    B. per sewer invert
    C. pounds per square inch
    D. pounds per sewer inlet

15. In order to increase culvert efficiency and to prevent undermining of the culvert, the entrance to the culvert is FREQUENTLY provided with a

    A. sump pump
    B. mud valve
    C. head wall
    D. scroll case

16. A sewer plan calls for pipe diameters of 3", 10", 12", 14", 15", and 18". The size which is NOT used for a standard strength clay sewer pipe is

    A. 10"   B. 12"   C. 14"   D. 15"

17. Lateral sanitary sewers should PREFERABLY intersect at a

    A. catch basin
    B. weir
    C. manhole
    D. tide gate

18. A dip, or sag, used in a sewer line to pass under structures, such as subways, is called a(n)

    A. outfall
    B. inverted siphon
    C. force main
    D. regulator

19. A device suitable for pumping sewage from deep basements into city sewers is a

    A. pressure relief valve
    B. vacuum breaker
    C. pneumatic ejector
    D. comminutor

20. The flow of ground water into sanitary sewers through defective joints is called

    A. back siphonage
    B. infiltration
    C. overflow
    D. exfiltration

21. In a combined sewer system, the amount of sewage flowing to the treatment plant is USUALLY controlled by a

    A. regulator
    B. bar screen
    C. siphon
    D. mud valve

22. The LOWEST portion of the inside of a sewer pipe is the

    A. crown
    B. haunch
    C. invert
    D. spring line

23. A.C pipe, sometimes used instead of clay sewer pipe, is made of

    A. reinforced concrete
    B. polyvinyl
    C. asbestos and cement
    D. asphalt

24. Of the following, the one which is NOT a sewer cleaning tool is the

    A. gouge
    B. wire brush
    C. pilaster
    D. claw

25. A sewer rodding machine has speeds up to 100 FPM. As used here, FPM is an abbreviation for feet per

    A. million
    B. mile
    C. minute
    D. module

KEY (CORRECT ANSWERS)

1.	B	11.	C
2.	D	12.	A
3.	A	13.	D
4.	D	14.	C
5.	D	15.	C
6.	C	16.	C
7.	B	17.	C
8.	B	18.	B
9.	D	19.	C
10.	B	20.	B

21. A
22. C
23. C
24. C
25. C

TEST 2

DIRECTIONS: Each question or incomplete statement is followed by several suggested answers or completions. Select the one that BEST answers the question or completes the statement. *PRINT THE LETTER OF THE CORRECT ANSWER IN THE SPACE AT THE RIGHT.*

1. Wellpoints are used in sewer construction PRIMARILY to   1.___
    - A. remove gases
    - B. dewater trenches
    - C. locate wells
    - D. replace hydrants

2. A sewer which carries only sewage from the plumbing fixtures in a house is a   2.___
    - A. storm sewer
    - B. combined sewer
    - C. sanitary sewer
    - D. subsurface drain

3. The slope of a sewer is MOST usually indicated by the units,   3.___
    - A. feet
    - B. rods
    - C. percent
    - D. diameters

4. Longitudinal timbers used to support the vertical sheeting in a sewer trench excavation are called   4.___
    - A. wales
    - B. cross braces
    - C. piles
    - D. cradles

5. The nominal diameter of a #4 reinforcing bar is MOST NEARLY   5.___
    - A. 0.4"
    - B. 0.04"
    - C. 0.5"
    - D. 4 mm

6. In a 1:2:3 concrete mix, the number 3 represents the proportion of   6.___
    - A. sand
    - B. water
    - C. coarse aggregate
    - D. cement

7. When investigating a complaint by a homeowner of sewage backing up in a house, you find that the house trap in the basement is blocked.
   Of the following, the PROPER action for you to take is to   7.___
    - A. call in a plumber for the homeowner
    - B. clean out the house trap
    - C. tell the homeowner to call in a plumber
    - D. disconnect the house trap from the piping, clean it out, and reinstall the trap

8. Your men should be careful not to break manhole covers.
   Of the following, the BEST reason for taking this precaution is that   8.___
    - A. the cost of the manhole cover will be taken out of your paycheck
    - B. the manhole cover can't be replaced
    - C. manhole covers cost money to replace
    - D. broken manhole covers are difficult to get rid of

9. You are to report immediately by telephone if a manhole cover or basin grate is missing. Of the following, the BEST reason for having this requirement is to

   A. permit the cover or grate to be ordered if it is not on hand
   B. be able to assess the responsibility for this condition
   C. prevent an accident
   D. enable the Sanitation Department to clean the street

10. Of the following, the LEAST serious of the defects filed in a sewer report is

   A. broken casting
   B. missing casting
   C. noisy manhole cover
   D. backed up sewer

11. Of the following, the BEST method for a foreman to use to teach a man how to lift a manhole cover safely is to

   A. tell him how to do it
   B. make a sketch showing the correct method to use
   C. actually lift a cover with the man watching
   D. let the man try to lift the cover and correct any mistakes

12. Assume that you are training a group of men on the adjustment of a high-pressure relief valve.
    Of the following, the FIRST topic you should discuss with the men is

   A. the conditions under which it is necessary to adjust the relief valve
   B. how to order parts for the relief valve
   C. how the springs in the relief valve work
   D. how to take apart the relief valve

13. If four men work seven hours during the day, the number of man-hours of work done is

   A. 4   B. 7   C. 11   D. 28

14. If it takes four men fourteen days to do a certain job, seven men, working at the same rate, should be able to do the same job in _____ days.

   A. 8   B. 7   C. 6   D. 5

15. A truck leaves the garage at 9:26 A.M. and returns the same day at 3:43 P.M. The period of time that the truck was away from the garage is MOST NEARLY _____ hours _____ minutes.

   A. 5; 17   B. 5; 43   C. 6; 17   D. 6; 26

16. The sum of 2 5/8, 3 3/16, 1 1/2, and 4 1/4 is

   A. 9 13/16   B. 10 7/16   C. 11 9/16   D. 13 3/16

17. Of the following, a procedure used for causing air to flow into and from the lungs of the body by mechanical or manual methods is called

   A. irrigation
   B. traction
   C. traumatic shock
   D. artificial respiration

18. The one of the following that is a toxic gas which is colorless and odorless is

    A. chlorine
    B. hydrogen sulfide
    C. carbon monoxide
    D. gasoline

19. In first aid, a tourniquet is MOST often used to

    A. improve respiration
    B. treat burns
    C. treat sprains
    D. control bleeding

20. Persons who have been injured may suffer a depressed condition of many of the body functions due to failure of enough blood to circulate through the body.
    This condition is called

    A. immunization
    B. chronic
    C. cathartic
    D. shock

21. The type of injury which is MOST likely to cause lockjaw (tetanus) is

    A. an epileptic convulsion
    B. a puncture wound
    C. an electric shock
    D. sunstroke

22. If filling out an accident form, there is a section entitled *Accident Type*.
    Of the following, the one that is an accident type is

    A. struck by falling object
    B. operated without authority
    C. worked too slowly
    D. engaged in horseplay

23. On an accident report, there is an item labeled *Nature of Injury*.
    Of the following, the one that belongs in this category is

    A. fracture
    B. carelessness
    C. defective equipment
    D. loose clothing

24. Assume that the men you supervise are cleaning out a catch basin and uncover a gun.
    Of the following, the BEST action to take is to

    A. notify the Police Department of the discovery
    B. throw the gun away because it probably does not work
    C. keep the gun since you may be able to repair it
    D. dismantle the gun before disposing of it because it may be loaded

25. Assume that a new piece of mechanical equipment is brought to the job.
    Of the following, the BEST way for the men to learn the proper use of the equipment is to

    A. have a representative of the company that manufactures the equipment come to the job and demonstrate its use
    B. let the men try out the equipment and learn the operation of the equipment by using it
    C. let the men read the instruction manual carefully before trying out the equipment
    D. deliver a lecture to the men that have to use the equipment on the proper use of the equipment

KEY (CORRECT ANSWERS)

1. B
2. C
3. C
4. A
5. C

6. C
7. C
8. C
9. C
10. C

11. C
12. A
13. D
14. A
15. C

16. C
17. D
18. C
19. D
20. D

21. B
22. A
23. A
24. A
25. A

———

EXAMINATION SECTION
TEST 1

DIRECTIONS: Each question or incomplete statement is followed by several suggested answers or completions. Select the one that BEST answers the question or completes the statement. *PRINT THE LETTER OF THE CORRECT ANSWER IN THE SPACE AT THE RIGHT.*

Questions 1-5.

DIRECTIONS: Questions 1 through 5, inclusive, refer to the distribution map shown on the LAST page of this test. All questions are to be answered in accordance with this map.

1. The symbol just west of the boundary gate symbol on 21st Street between Willow Avenue and Meadow Avenue is a

   A. hydrant
   B. gate valve
   C. check valve
   D. reducer

   1_____

2. The number of hydrants on the 30" main in Meadow Avenue between 22nd Street and 23rd Street is

   A. none   B. 1   C. 2   D. 3

   2_____

3. The *S* symbol on the main at the west end of 18th Street means that the main is

   A. a special casting
   B. made of steel
   C. shut down
   D. high pressure service

   3_____

4. A cap is located at or near the intersection of _____ Street and _____ Avenue.

   A. 24th; Willow
   B. 22nd; Willow
   C. 26th; Meadow
   D. 21st; Central

   4_____

5. A blow off is located in

   A. Meadow Avenue between 19th & 20th Streets
   B. 22nd Street between Willow Avenue and Meadow Avenue
   C. Wilen Avenue between 22nd and 23rd Streets
   D. 22nd Street between Willow Avenue and Central Avenue

   5_____

6. Assume that a normally sober man appears on the job intoxicated. Of the following, the BEST procedure for a foreman to follow is to

   A. give the man an easy job so that he cannot get hurt
   B. let the man *sleep it off* in the morning and put him to work in the afternoon
   C. let the man work at his normal duties but keep an *eye* on him
   D. send him home for the day

   6_____

7. The Chief Engineer has decided to change the procedure that must be followed in making certain types of repairs. The one of the following statements concerning the new procedure that is CORRECT is:
The men

   7_____

A. should know why the procedure is being changed because they will then be more interested in the job
B. do not have to know the reason for the change because they need do only the work as they are told
C. should know why the procedure is being changed so that they can decide which method of doing the job is better
D. do not have to know the reason for the change because they are not capable of judging the best method of doing a job

8. A foreman, by mistake, orders his men to do a job improperly.
Of the following, the BEST thing for the foreman to do when he realizes his error is to

A. insist that the job be done as he ordered so that his mistake will not be discovered
B. admit that he made the mistake and correct the order
C. tell the men that the order came from *higher up so* that he will not be blamed for the mistake
D. tell the men that he is merely trying this out to see if it works better

9. The BEST foreman is usually the

A. fastest worker
B. man who is most familiar with the streets in the borough
C. strongest man
D. man who is most tactful

10. A good foreman will

A. look after the welfare of his men
B. demand perfection in the work of his men at all times
C. make special efforts to impress his superiors
D. cover up for the actions of his men

11. As a newly appointed foreman, it is MOST important that you

A. show the men who is boss by issuing orders
B. prove to the men that you know more than they do
C. become acquainted with the men and their abilities
D. show the men how friendly you are

12. A foreman who criticizes his department head is a

A. *good* foreman, because the men will feel he is on their side
B. *poor* foreman, because the men will lose respect for him
C. *good* foreman, because he will get more work done
D. *poor* foreman, because he will have no time to do his own work

13. One of the men in your gang comes to you, the foreman, and complains that the men in the gang have taken a dislike to him and are making trouble for him.
Of the following, the BEST thing for you to do is to

A. tell the man he must learn to get along with the other men
B. report the matter to your superior
C. call the gang together and tell them they must stop making trouble
D. investigate the complaint to determine what the problem is

14. As a foreman, you are inspecting the damage done by water from a broken main leaking into the basement of a store. After inspecting the damage, the owner complains to you about the conduct of the men who made the repair.
Of the following, the BEST way of handling this situation is to tell the owner that

    A. you are there to inspect the damage to the premises only
    B. he should make his complaint to higher authorities
    C. his complaint will be investigated and, if found correct, proper action will be taken
    D. nothing can be done at this time since the men are no longer at this location

14____

Questions 15-17.

DIRECTIONS: Questions 15 through 17, inclusive, are based on the paragraph below. These questions are to be answered in accordance with the information given in this paragraph.

Excavation of trench. The trench shall be excavated as directed; one side of the street or avenue shall be left open for traffic at all times. In paved streets, the length of trench that may be opened between the point where the backfilling has been completed and the point where the pavement is being removed shall not exceed fifteen hundred feet for pipes 24 inches or less in diameter. For pipes larger than 24 inch, the length of open trenches shall not exceed one thousand feet. The completion of the backfilling shall be interpreted to mean the backfilling of the trench and the consolidation of the backfill so that vehicular traffic can be resumed over the backfill, and also the placing of any temporary pavement that *may* be required.

15. According to the above paragraph, the street

    A. can be closed to traffic in emergencies
    B. can be closed to traffic only when laying more than 1500 feet of pipe
    C. is closed to traffic as directed
    D. shall be left open for traffic at all times

15____

16. According to the above paragraph, the MAXIMUM length of open trench permitted in paved streets depends on the

    A. traffic on the street
    B. type of ground that is being excaVated
    C. water conditions met with in excavation
    D. diameter of the pipe being laid

16____

17. According to the above paragraph, the one of the following items that is included in the *completion of the back-filling* is

    A. sheeting and bracing   B. cradle
    C. temporary pavement   D. bridging

17____

Questions 18-20.

DIRECTIONS: Questions 18 through 20, inclusive, are based on the paragraph below. These questions are to be answered in accordance with the information given in this paragraph.

The Contractor shall notify the Engineer by noon of the day immediately preceding the date when he wishes to shut down any main, and if the time set be approved, the Contractor shall provide the men necessary to shut down the main at the time stipulated, and to previously notify all consumers whose supply may be affected. These men shall be under the direction of the Department employees, who will superintend all operations of valves and hydrants. Shutdowns for making connections will not be made unless and until the Contractor has everything on the ground in readiness for the work.

18. According to the above paragraph, before a contractor can make a shut-down, he MUST notify the

    A. Police Department
    B. district foreman
    C. engineer
    D. highway department

19. According to the above paragraph, the operation of the valves will be supervised by the

    A. department employees
    B. contractor's men
    C. contractor's superintendent
    D. engineer

20. According to the above paragraph, shut-downs for connections are made

    A. the day before the connection is made
    B. first and then consumers are notified
    C. at any time convenient to the contractor
    D. when the contractor has everything on the ground in readiness for the work

21. Water hammer in a pipe line is MOST frequently caused by _____ a valve too _____ .

    A. opening; rapidly
    B. opening; slowly
    C. closing; rapidly
    D. closing; slowly

22. In using a hacksaw, pressure should be applied to the hacksaw when

    A. pushing it
    B. pulling it
    C. pushing and pulling it
    D. either pushing or pulling, depending upon the way the cut is to be made

23. When cutting cast iron (other than pipe) with a hacksaw, the PROPER number of teeth per inch in the blade should be

    A. 14   B. 18   C. 24   D. 32

24. Concrete is a mixture of cement and

    A. lime, sand, and water
    B. sand and water
    C. sand and broken stone
    D. sand, broken stone, and water

25. The head of a cold chisel has mushroomed after considerable use. 25____
 The BEST thing to do is

 A. continue to use it since mushrooming is normal
 B. throw it away
 C. send it to the shop for redressing
 D. use a file to restore the head to its original shape

26. A valve box cover has been covered with asphalt during a street repaving job. 26____
 The BEST way to locate the valve is to use a

 A. geophone
 B. aquaphone
 C. distribution map and a tape
 D. probing bar

27. The number of cubic yards in a bin 4 feet by 8 feet by 13 feet is MOST NEARLY _____ 27____
 cubic yards.

 A. 17   B. 15   C. 13   D. 11

28. The letter *P* stencilled on the roadside face of a hydrant indicates that the hydrant 28____

 A. is a low pressure hydrant
 B. is a high pressure hydrant
 C. is out of service permanently
 D. has a plugged drain

29. A hydrant extension piece would MOST likely be used if 29____

 A. the hydrant had been damaged
 B. an open trench exists in the street in front of the hydrant
 C. several hose lines must be connected to the hydrant
 D. the hose connections do not fit the hydrant nozzles

30. The drip valve of a hydrant 30____

 A. should not open until after the hydrant valve has closed
 B. should open just before the hydrant valve has closed
 C. operates completely independent of the operation of the hydrant valve
 D. should only be closed during repair of the hydrant

31. To remove and replace the operating parts of a hydrant which is in service, 31____

 A. the standpipe must be disconnected from the elbow
 B. it is necessary to do some excavating
 C. the main must be shut down
 D. no excavation is necessary

32. The material generally used for packing hydrant stems is 32____

 A. asbestos   B. rubber cloth
 C. flax   D. leather

33. A roundabout would normally have as a component part a

    A. four-way   B. valve   C. plug   D. cap

34. Cast iron reducers are usually made in all but one of the following ways. The way in which they are NOT made is

    A. spigots on both ends
    B. hub on large end, spigot on small end
    C. hub on small end, spigot on large end
    D. hubs on both ends

35. A cast iron main running due east is to turn so that it runs N45W, that is, halfway between north and west. The change in direction could be made using _____ bends.

    A. sixteen 1/48
    B. six 1/16
    C. four 1/8
    D. two 1/4

36. A cast iron offset would NORMALLY be used

    A. to change the direction of a main
    B. when the main must run diagonally from one side of the street to the other
    C. when the main must be shifted parallel to itself several feet to avoid an existing structure
    D. when the main must be shifted several inches to avoid an existing structure

37. A 30-inch cast iron main is to be laid with a blow-off and an air cock. The cast iron piece used for the blow-off differs from that used for the air cock in

    A. size of outlet
    B. general shape
    C. material used
    D. length measured along the main

38. The upper part of a standard hydrant valve box is USUALLY connected to the lower part by

    A. screw threads   B. bolts
    C. a beaded rim   D. lugs and rods

39. A trench for an 18-inch cast iron main is being excavated in rock. The width of the trench should be AT LEAST _____ inches.

    A. 30   B. 36   C. 42   D. 48

40. Specifications of the Department of Water Supply, Gas and Electricity state that in a trench excavated in rock, projections of rock must be removed if they come within a certain distance of the outside of any portion of the pipe barrel or bell. This distance is, in inches,

    A. 4   B. 6   C. 8   D. 10

KEY (CORRECT ANSWERS)

1. D	11. C	21. C	31. D
2. A	12. B	22. A	32. C
3. B	13. D	23. B	33. B
4. D	14. C	24. D	34. D
5. D	15. D	25. C	35. B
6. D	16. D	26. C	36. D
7. A	17. C	27. B	37. A
8. B	18. C	28. D	38. A
9. D	19. A	29. B	39. C
10. A	20. D	30. A	40. B

8 (#1)

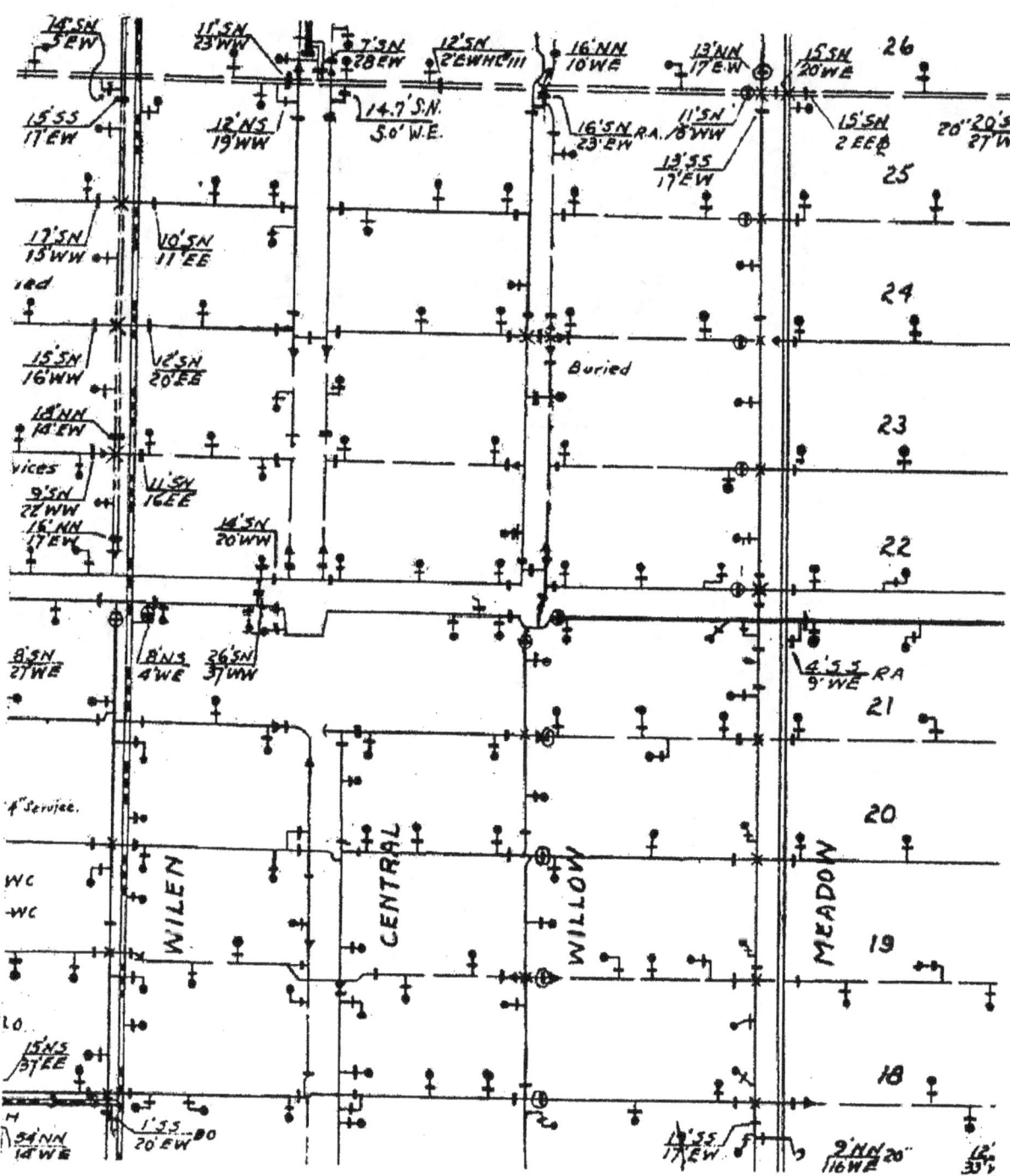

TEST 2

DIRECTIONS: Each question or incomplete statement is followed by several suggested answers or completions. Select the one that BEST answers the question or completes the statement. *PRINT THE LETTER OF THE CORRECT ANSWER IN THE SPACE AT THE RIGHT.*

1. The MAXIMUM size of stones permitted in backfill is _____ inches. 1____
   A. 12   B. 8   C. 4   D. 2

2. A two-inch galvanized steel pipe is to be connected to a cast iron main. 2____
   The connection should be made by a standard corporation tap of the following size: _____ inch.
   A. 1   B. 1 1/2   C. 2   D. 2 1/2

3. Standard cast iron pipe of inside diameter from 12 to 20 inches may be furnished in nominal laying lengths up to and including _____ feet. 3____
   A. 14   B. 16   C. 18   D. 20

4. The interior surface of new 12-inch cast iron pipe is USUALLY coated with 4____
   A. cement mortar   B. nothing
   C. asphalt paint   D. coal tar pitch

5. A tarpaulin would MOST likely be used when 5____
   A. mixing concrete
   B. running lead joints
   C. lowering pipe into a trench
   D. excavating a trench for a water main

6. Bands and bolts would be LEAST likely to be required at 6____
   A. bends   B. branches   C. plugs   D. four-ways

7. A house service with a 3/8-inch tap on an existing main is to be transferred to a new main. 7____
   The size of the tap on the new main should be _____ inch.
   A. 5/8   B. 1/2   C. 3/8   D. 1/4

8. The LARGEST tap permitted on a new 12-inch main is _____ inch. 8____
   A. 1   B. 1 1/2   C. 2   D. 2 1/2

9. The sheeting of a trench serves 9____
   A. only to protect workmen
   B. only to prevent damage to existing mains close to the trench
   C. only to prevent damage to pavement
   D. all three of the foregoing purposes

10. Water required for flushing backfill is USUALLY supplied

    A. in a fine spray
    B. by an ordinary garden hose
    C. from a tank truck
    D. through a flushing pipe

11. Water mains are USUALLY laid parallel to the curb at a distance of APPROXIMATELY _____ feet.

    A. 15   B. 12   C. 9   D. 6

12. After a main has been laid but prior to putting it into service, it should be disinfected by

    A. continuous flushing with water containing chlorine
    B. continuous flushing with clean water only
    C. introducing chlorine into the water in the pipe and letting the solution stand for 30 minutes
    D. blowing chlorine gas through the main

13. Before trimming a caulked pipe joint, the lead of a lead joint should

    A. extend outside the face of the bell
    B. be flush with the face of the bell
    C. be inside the face of the bell
    D. be heated

14. Drainage of hydrants require the use of lead lined pipe

    A. except when a cast iron drain base is provided
    B. except when the hydrant is connected to a sewer
    C. except when a blind drain is provided
    D. in every case

15. A standard cast iron reducer is to connect a 24-inch main to a smaller main. The length of the reducer USUALLY

    A. is the same regardless of the size of the smaller main
    B. decreases as the size of the smaller main decreases
    C. increases as the size of the smaller main decreases
    D. can be varied to fit the field conditions

16. A standard cast iron three-way does NOT have more than the following number of hubs:

    A. 3   B. 2   C. 1   D. 0

17. Of the following statements, the one which is CORRECT is:

    A. A cap is used on the spigot end of a pipe
    B. A plug is used on the spigot end of a pipe
    C. Caps and plugs can be used interchangeably
    D. Caps are usually available in larger sizes than plugs

3 (#2)

18. Of the following statements, the one which is CORRECT is:

    A. A planned shutdown is not made rapidly
    B. In the event of an emergency shutdown, all valves in the area should be closed and then a study of the distribution map should be made to determine which valves can be opened
    C. Boundary gates should always be kept closed for the duration of an emergency shutdown
    D. The operation of all valves to be used in a planned shutdown should be checked prior to making the shutdown

18_____

19. When building material is stored on the street for the construction of a building,

    A. the Department of Water Supply, Gas and Electricity is not concerned
    B. there can be no objections if hydrants are accessible
    C. there can be no objections if the storage period is short
    D. serious difficulties for the Department of Water Supply, Gas and Electricity could result

19_____

20. A large steel main is to be emptied through a blow-off. The BEST way to proceed is to open

    A. the blow-off
    B. an aircock or hydrant at the high point of the main before opening the blow-off
    C. the blow-off and then open an air cock or hydrant at the high point of the main
    D. an air cock or hydrant at the low point of the main before opening the blow-off

20_____

21. A large new main is to be placed in service.
    To fill the main, it is important to FIRST open

    A. the head gate valve
    B. an air cock or hydrant on the main
    C. all side gate valves
    D. the side gate valves on one side of the main only

21_____

22. Of the following special castings, the one which is MOST like a blow-off is a

    A. four-way   B. reducer   C. three-way   D. offset

22_____

23. The laying length of a double hub

    A. is less than one foot
    B. depends upon the diameter of the pipe
    C. must be at least nine feet
    D. may be any length up to 20 feet, the maximum length depending upon the diameter

23_____

24. The gooseneck that is GENERALLY used to connect a service pipe to a main

    A. should be straight for its entire length
    B. comes in a standard length and, therefore, must be curved to make it fit

24_____

C. is deliberately curved so that it can accommodate movement between main and service pipe
D. is curved to provide extra length so that it can be cut and still be long enough to reconnect to the main

25. A non-rising stem gate valve would MOST likely be used when

    A. the threads of the stem must be readily accessible for lubrication
    B. space is limited
    C. the valve is used infrequently
    D. the valve is in a deep valve vault

26. Of the following types of valves, the one which is NOT usually found on water mains is the _____ valve.

    A. glove   B. air relief
    C. pressure regulating   D. gate

27. When a length of cast iron pipe is too long, it is USUALLY cut with a(n)

    A. chisel   B. hacksaw
    C. emery wheel   D. cutting torch

28. The PRINCIPAL objection to laying mains between December 15 and March 15 is with the

    A. freezing of water
    B. working conditions for the men
    C. freezing of soil
    D. the reduced length of daylight

29. A trench for a cast iron main is USUALLY backfilled immediately

    A. after the joints are caulked
    B. after the pressure test has been completed
    C. before water is placed in the main
    D. after water is placed in the main

30. When the pavement along the sides of a trench becomes undermined, the BEST thing to do is

    A. carefully tamp the backfill under the undermined pavement
    B. place a layer of broken stone on top of the backfill under the undermined pavement
    C. break down the undermined pavement before backfilling
    D. consolidate the backfill by thorough flushing

31. A small leak in a main would usually be MOST serious in the

    A. summer   B. fall   C. spring   D. winter

32. When sheeting for a trench is not to be removed before backfilling, the sheeting should be driven or cut off so that it

    A. is flush with the surface of the ground
    B. is at least 8 inches below the surface of the ground

C. will project at least two inches into the pavement base
D. is flush with the top surface of the pavement base

33. While excavating a trench in rock by blasting, a water main which crosses the line of the trench is uncovered. Of the following methods, the BEST one for continuing the rock excavation in the vicinity of the main is

   A. shut down the main
   B. place blasting mats to cover the main
   C. use lighter blasting charges
   D. relocate the main temporarily so that it is outside the danger area of the building

34. When the bottom of a trench for a water main is in rock, the pipe should be permanently supported on

   A. clean earth backfill which is tamped
   B. wooden blocking
   C. sand backfill which is flushed
   D. concreted cradles

35. On which one of the following days of the week should a planned shutdown normally be made?

   A. Sunday
   B. Monday
   C. Tuesday
   D. Wednesday

36. Permissible leakage during a field test is two (2) gallons per linear foot of pipe joint per 24 hours.
    For a 24-inch main, 1,000 feet long, with 16-foot laying lengths, the permissible leakage in 24 hours is, in gallons, MOST NEARLY

   A. 750
   B. 770
   C. 790
   D. 810

37. Contract limitations on the maximum quantities of materials that may be delivered to the site, and on the time of such deliveries, are USUALLY made in order to

   A. insure the completion of the work on schedule
   B. prevent the contractor from asking for an extension of time because materials were not available
   C. reduce congestion at the site of the work
   D. protect the manufacturer supplying the material

38. Steel reinforcing bars for reinforced concrete should

   A. be painted with red lead
   B. be painted with asphalt paint
   C. be painted with oil paint
   D. not be painted

39. Steel water mains are lined with

   A. coal tar enamel only
   B. coal tar enamel or cement mortar
   C. cement mortar only
   D. nothing

40. The principal danger in NOT opening an air cock when draining a main is that the main might

   A. not empty
   B. only partly empty
   C. empty too fast
   D. collapse

KEY (CORRECT ANSWERS)

1. C	11. C	21. B	31. D
2. B	12. A	22. C	32. B
3. D	13. A	23. A	33. D
4. A	14. D	24. C	34. D
5. C	15. C	25. B	35. D
6. D	16. B	26. A	36. C
7. A	17. A	27. A	37. C
8. C	18. D	28. C	38. D
9. D	19. D	29. A	39. B
10. D	20. B	30. C	40. D

EXAMINATION SECTION
TEST 1

DIRECTIONS: Each question or incomplete statement is followed by several suggested answers or completions. Select the one that BEST answers the question or completes the statement. *PRINT THE LETTER OF THE CORRECT ANSWER IN THE SPACE AT THE RIGHT.*

1. A Bourdon tube gage is used to measure

    A. temperature
    B. acidity
    C. turbidity
    D. pressure

2. An instrument used to locate buried metallic pipes is known as a(n)

    A. scleroscope
    B. M-scope
    C. kinoscope
    D. oscilloscope

3. The PRIMARY function of a check valve is to

    A. prevent the illegal use of fire hydrants
    B. insure adequate water pressure in high buildings
    C. prevent freezing of water
    D. permit flow of water in one direction only

4. Of the following, the torque applied by a ratchet wrench would be expressed in units of

    A. horsepower
    B. pounds
    C. pounds per square inch
    D. foot-pounds

5. Most lead joints runners are made of

    A. nylon
    B. asbestos
    C. leadite
    D. polyethylene

6. The tool shown in the sketch at the right is a

    A. pickout iron
    B. pipe jointer
    C. cover bolt wrench
    D. pipe reamer

7. In order to reduce the force necessary to open or close large gate valves, the valves are equipped with a

    A. vacuum breaker
    B. by-pass
    C. saddle
    D. shear gate

8. In order to open a ground-key valve, used as a corporation cock to full flow, it is necessary to rotate the handle _____ degrees.

    A. 45
    B. 60
    C. 75
    D. 90

9. A foot valve is MOST often used

   A. to relieve excess pressure in a water main
   B. on the suction pipe of a centrifugal pump
   C. at the high point in a pipeline
   D. to drain a pipeline

10. Of the following tools, the one that generally should NOT be used to tighten screwed piping is a _____ wrench.

    A. Stillson   B. strap
    C. monkey   D. chain

11. A 6-inch branch may be connected to an 8-inch main without shutting off the flow of water by using a

    A. tapping valve and sleeve
    B. cutting in tee
    C. cutting in valve and sleeve
    D. pipe tong

12. When water flows through a thirty-second bend, the direction of flow changes

    A. 11 1/4°   B. 22 1/2°   C. 45°   D. 90°

13. A main in which water is flowing east is connected to a pipe offset. As the water leaves the offset, it will be flowing toward the

    A. north   B. south   C. east   D. west

14. An electrolysis test connection on a water main is used to measure the

    A. salinity of the ground water outside the main
    B. the chlorine residual in the water in the main
    C. stray electric current in the main
    D. temperature of the ground around the main

15. A common method of temporarily lowering the ground water below the level of operations in a trench is by the use of

    A. wellpoints   B. mud valves
    C. piles   D. trenching machines

16. The diameter of a #6 steel reinforcing bar is MOST NEARLY

    A. 1"   B. 3/4"   C. 1/2"   D. 1/4"

17. The quick opening or closing of valves or gates, and the sudden starting, stopping, or variation in speed of pumps is FREQUENTLY the cause of

    A. sluggish flow of water   B. water-borne diseases
    C. water hammer   D. water hardness

18. Poured lead pipe joints must be calked MAINLY because the hot lead

    A. corrodes some of the cast iron   B. burns some of the jute
    C. becomes porous on cooling   D. shrinks on cooling

19. Flexibility between a water main and a service pipe can be obtained by the use of a

   A. corporation cock
   B. gooseneck
   C. curb stop
   D. air-release valve

20. It is necessary to shut off the water in a main temporarily in order to make repairs. In order to get cooperation from the general public, the

   A. job should be done at night so that few people will be aware of it
   B. shut-off crew should be ordered not to speak to the general public
   C. job should be done in several stages so that the public realizes how difficult the problem is
   D. purpose and duration of the shut-off should be explained to the general public

Questions 21-25.

DIRECTIONS: Questions 21 through 25 are to be answered on the basis of maps or diagrams used by departments of water resources.

21. On a distribution map, the symbol ——— — ——— refers to a main whose diameter is

   A. 6"
   B. 8"
   C. 10"
   D. 12"

22. On a distribution map, the symbol refers to a

   A. gate valve
   B. blow-off
   C. air-cock
   D. regulator

23. On a distribution map, the symbol refers to a

   A. gate valve
   B. 3-way
   C. 4-way
   D. reducer

24. On a distribution map, the symbol refers to a

   A. hydrant
   B. air-cock
   C. 3-way
   D. 4-way

25. On a work area diagram, the symbol refers to a(n)

   A. office
   B. truck
   C. barricade
   D. excavation.

KEY (CORRECT ANSWERS)

1.	D	11.	A
2.	B	12.	A
3.	D	13.	C
4.	D	14.	C
5.	B	15.	A
6.	D	16.	B
7.	B	17.	C
8.	D	18.	D
9.	B	19.	B
10.	C	20.	D

21. B
22. B
23. A
24. C
25. D

TEST 2

DIRECTIONS: Each question or incomplete statement is followed by several suggested answers or completions. Select the one that BEST answers the question or completes the statement. *PRINT THE LETTER OF THE CORRECT ANSWER IN THE SPACE AT THE RIGHT.*

1. According to standard water main specifications, prior to laying any straight pipe or special castings, the inside surfaces shall be mopped or sprayed with a chlorine solution containing not less than 150 _____ of chlorine. 1._____

    A. quarts   B. lbs.   C. p.p.m.   D. tanks

2. When water main repairs are underway on the north side of a two-way street which runs east and west, the location recommended by the Department of Water Resources of a lead heating burner is _____ of the excavation. 2._____

    A. north   B. east   C. south   D. west

3. Of the following statements, the one which is NOT included on the official water supply shut-off notice is 3._____

    A. turn off water-cooled refrigerating and air conditioning units
    B. close main house valve on water pipe supplying premises
    C. drain all water pipes above the basement
    D. open, as a vent, one hot water faucet above the level of the hot water storage tank

4. In order to obtain a Temporary Street Opening Permit, the applicant must be a 4._____

    A. city resident   B. city employee
    C. licensed plumber   D. professional engineer

5. In accordance with standard water main specifications, all water mains 20 inches in diameter or larger shall be subjected to a leakage test at a pressure of 125 psi. The leakage shall NOT be greater than 5._____

    A. twenty gallons per 24 hours
    B. two gallons per linear foot of pipe joint per 24 hours
    C. two gallons per linear foot of pipe joint per 20 minutes
    D. twenty gallons per mile of pipe per 24 hours

6. In accordance with official specifications, in paved streets the length of trench that may be opened between the point where the backfilling has been completed and the point where the pavement is being removed shall NOT exceed 6._____

    A. the width of the street
    B. fifteen hundred feet for pipes 24 inches or less in diameter
    C. five hundred feet for all pipe diameters
    D. the distance between hydrants

Questions 7-10.

DIRECTIONS: Questions 7 through 10 are to be answered SOLELY on the basis of the following passage.

The choice of equipment to be used in excavating a trench will depend on the job conditions, the depth and width of the trench, the class of the soil, the extent to which ground water is present, the width of the right of way for the disposal of excavated earth, and the type of equipment already owned by a contractor.

If a relatively shallow and narrow trench is to be excavated in firm soil, the wheel-type trenching machine is probably the most suitable. However, if the soil is rock, which requires blasting, the most suitable excavator will be a hoe, or a less desirable substitute could be a dragline. If the soil is unstable, water-saturated material, it may be necessary to use a dragline, hoe, or clamshell and let the walls establish a stable slope. If it is necessary to install solid sheeting to hold the walls in place, neither a hoe nor a dragline will work satisfactorily. A clamshell, which can excavate between the trench braces that hold the sheeting in place, probably will be the best equipment for the job.

7. According to the above passage, the wheel-type trenching machine is probably the MOST suitable for excavating

   A. unstable, water-saturated material
   B. when it is necessary to install solid sheeting
   C. a relatively shallow and narrow trench in firm soil
   D. when ground water is present

8. According to the above passage, the width of the right of way for the disposal of excavated earth

   A. depends upon the width of the street
   B. affects the depth of cover
   C. affects the choice of equipment to be used in excavating
   D. should be minimized to avoid inconveniencing the public

9. According to the above passage, a hoe will be the MOST suitable excavator if the

   A. soil is rock which requires blasting
   B. equipment is already owned by a contractor
   C. trench requires solid sheeting
   D. trench is over twenty feet deep

10. According to the above passage, the BEST equipment to use for excavating when it is necessary to install solid sheeting to hold the walls in place probably will be a

    A. clamshell
    B. dragline
    C. hoe
    D. wheel-type trenching machine

Questions 11-12.

DIRECTIONS: Questions 11 and 12 are to be answered SOLELY on the basis of the following passage.

Construction pumps frequently are required to perform under severe conditions, such as resulting from variations in the pumping head or from handling water that is muddy, sandy and trashy, or highly corrosive. The rate of pumping may vary several hundred percent during the period of construction. The most satisfactory solution to the pumping problem may be a single all-purpose pump, or it may be to use several types and sizes of pumps, to permit flexibility in the operations. The proper solution is to select the equipment which will take care of the pumping needs adequately at the lowest total cost.

11. According to the above passage, the PROPER solution to a construction pumping problem is to select equipment that has the lowest total cost which will also   11._____

   A. perform under severe conditions
   B. take care of the pumping needs adequately
   C. permit flexibility in operations
   D. provide maximum safety

12. According to the above passage, a variation of several hundred percent during the period of construction may occur in the   12._____

   A. pumping head
   B. rate of pumping
   C. volume of sandy and trashy water
   D. volume of highly corrosive water

Questions 13-14.

DIRECTIONS: Questions 13 and 14 are to be answered SOLELY on the basis of the following passage.

The mechanical failure of equipment may be the cause of a serious accident. Competent maintenance of equipment will reduce mechanical failures and in so doing reduce injuries and construction interruptions. Regular inspection of equipment will reduce maintenance expense.

13. Of the following, the BEST title for the above passage is   13._____

   A. Construction Productivity
   B. Preventive Maintenance of Equipment
   C. Inspection of Equipment
   D. Economical Construction

14. According to the above passage, the way to save money in construction work is to   14._____

   A. have qualified people operate equipment
   B. have periodic inspection of equipment
   C. have regular overhaul of equipment
   D. start a maintenance training program

15. Of the following items, the one MOST suitable for measuring the flow of water in a pipe is a   15._____

   A. poppet   B. hydraulic ram
   C. cistern   D. pitometer

16.

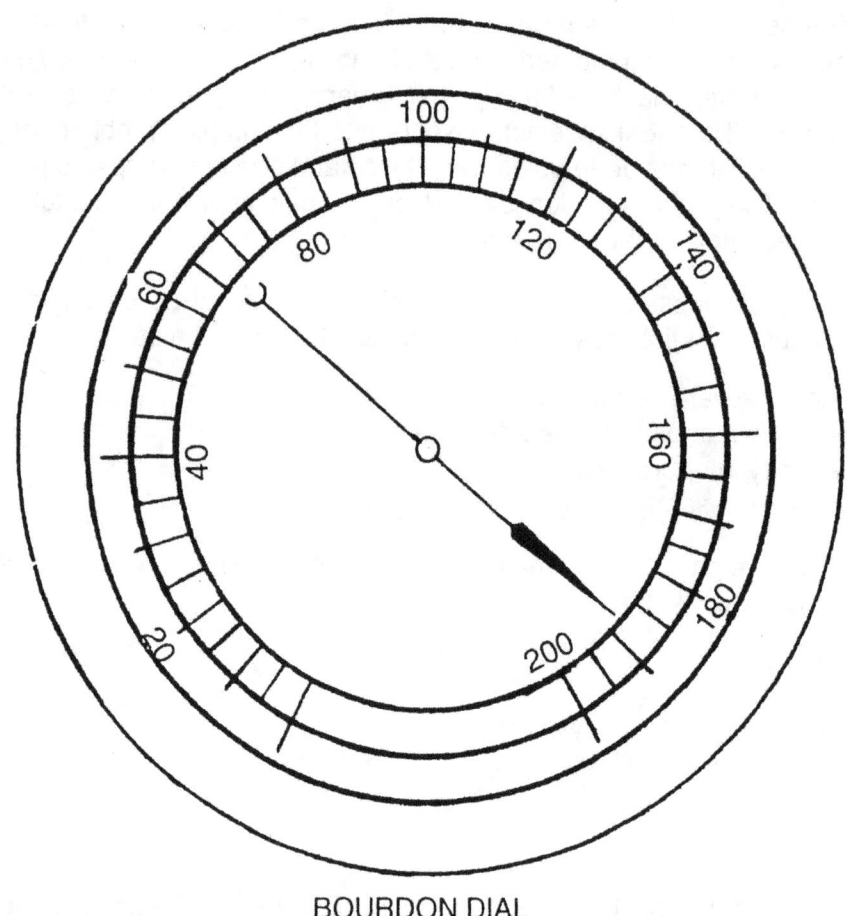

BOURDON DIAL

The reading indicated on the above dial is MOST NEARLY

A. 183   B. 188   C. 192   D. 196

17. An instrument used for detecting the sound of flowing water in a pipe network is a(n)

A. micrometer   B. spectrometer
C. aquaphone   D. viscophone

18. Of the following, the MAIN purpose of a Venturi meter is to measure the _____ in a main.

A. quantity of water flowing
B. chlorine content of the water
C. velocity of the water
D. temperature of the water

19. A blade with a small hole in the tip, used for measuring the flow from a hydrant, is a

A. hydrant pitot   B. Venturi meter
C. parshall flume   D. hydrant head

20. Hydrant-flow tests include observation of the pressure at a centrally situated hydrant and measurement of

    A. pressure at a group of neighboring hydrants
    B. flow from outlets at the top floor of a building
    C. reservoir elevation
    D. flow from a group of neighboring hydrants

21. Of the following, the one which is NOT a requirement of a satisfactory report is that it should be

    A. timely   B. lengthy   C. legible   D. accurate

22. When an accident occurs, the FIRST concern of the Foreman should be to

    A. see that injured person is properly cared for
    B. make sketches of the area
    C. interview the injured person
    D. interview witnesses and coworkers

23. Workers whose characteristics and behavior are such as to make them considerably more liable to injury than the average person are considered to be

    A. late
    B. safety conscious
    C. careful
    D. accident-prone

24. Safety inspections are not useful in an accident prevention program unless

    A. all persons who have accidents are fined
    B. insurance rates are decreased
    C. immediate action is taken to correct the conditions revealed
    D. there is adequate compensation for all injured parties

25. A Foreman is BEST qualified to investigate accidents involving his subordinates because he

    A. has all safety equipment for the job
    B. has more free time than his superiors
    C. has more skill than his superiors
    D. is familiar with all the job conditions

KEY (CORRECT ANSWERS)

1. C
2. D
3. C
4. C
5. B

6. B
7. C
8. C
9. A
10. A

11. B
12. B
13. B
14. B
15. D

16. B
17. C
18. A
19. A
20. D

21. B
22. A
23. D
24. C
25. D

EXAMINATION SECTION
TEST 1

DIRECTIONS: Directly and concisely, using brief answer form, answer the following questions.

1. What is put over block to give the cement something to stick to?
2. What insulating material is usually used, to protect water pipes against freezing?
3. What is the usual thickness of the cement as applied over flange fittings?
4. What material is used as a jacket over flange fittings?
5. What material is used as a covering on ammonia or brine piping?
6. What material is put over the hair felt on brine pipe?
7. What material is used as a joint filler or seal on brine pipe insulation?
8. What is put on after the magnesia blocks are in place?
9. What are four kinds of insulating material commonly used on piping?
10. If wires are used, how many are used between sections?

2 (#1)

KEY (CORRECT ANSWERS)

1. Chicken wire (wire mesh)

2. Hair felt

3. 1/2 to 1 inch

4. Canvas
   Drill

5. Hair felt
   Cork

6. Tar paper
   Canvas

7. Seam filler
   Brine putty
   Ground cork and pitch

8. Cement
   Wire

9. Air cell
   Wool felt
   Cork
   Magnesia
   Asbestos
   Hair felt

10. 3 to 6 wires

———

TEST 2

DIRECTIONS: Directly and concisely, using brief answer form, answer the following questions.

1. What is the covering placed on low temperature piping called?
2. With what material are molded cork contact joints sealed?
3. When using a sail needle, what is used to take the place of a thimble?
4. What insulation is used on high-pressure steam pipes which are subjected to vibration and to temperatures up to 700 degrees Fahrenheit?
5. What is used to join lengths of galvanized steel pipe?
6. What determines the thickness of insulating material to be put on a steam system?
7. In stitching canvas covering over pipes, where is the seam run?
8. What kind of nails (not size) are used on cork insulation work?
9. What is done to granulated cork to make cork pipe covering?
10. What is the LEAST number of wires used on flanged and screwed fittings over 6 inches in size?

KEY (CORRECT ANSWERS)

1. Air cell

2. Waterproof cement
   Seam filler
   Brine putty

3. Palm

4. High temperature (high temp.)
   Sponge felt
   Magnesia

5. Threaded ends and sealer

6. Steam pressure
   Temperature

7. Out of sight
   Back or top of pipe

8. Galvanized nails
   Wooden skewers

9. Compressed (molded and baked)

10. Three to six wires

TEST 3

DIRECTIONS: Directly and concisely, using brief answer form, answer the following questions.

1. What is used to insulate flanged fittings?
2. What material is used as an insulation jacket on boilers?
3. Where does one start placing the membrane jacket on straight pipe?
4. What is the length of the stitches used on canvas covering?
5. What sections of molded cork is used together?
6. What material is put between the canvas covering and the asbestos?
7. What material is put on first when covering steam boilers with asbestos insulation?
8. What kind of joints are used between courses on a sheet cork insulated wall that is to be plastered?
9. What material is used to attach sheet insulation to sheet metal?
10. What material is used to anchor a tie to sheet cork that is being used on furring or on one side of a free standing wall?

KEY (CORRECT ANSWERS)

1. Asbestos block

2. Magnesia block
   Canvas

3. At a fitting

4. 1/2 inch
   2 or 3 to the inch

5. Mated (fitted) (matched)

6. Building paper (tar paper)

7. Magnesia blocks

8. Broken (staggered)
   Open

9. Screws
   Wire
   Adhestive (asphalt) (pitch)

10. Nails
    Pitch
    Asbestos cement

EXAMINATION SECTION
TEST 1

DIRECTIONS: Each question or incomplete statement is followed by several suggested answers or completions. Select the one that BEST answers the question or completes the statement. *PRINT THE LETTER OF THE CORRECT ANSWER IN THE SPACE AT THE RIGHT.*

1. Of the following, the MOST important objective in accident analysis is to determine 1._____

    A. who is to blame
    B. how the accident could have been prevented
    C. whether the injured persons had received prescribed medical treatment
    D. the names of the persons involved and the exact nature of the injuries

2. Of the following statements, the one which would be of LEAST help in getting your men to do their work safely is to 2._____

    A. correct their unsafe work habits only if you think they may cause an accident
    B. see that they read and understand the safety rules they should follow
    C. talk to them often about the important of following safety regulations
    D. watch them at all times when they are working to see that they observe safety rules

3. The safety experts in your agency want to study accident reports as they are submitted in order to learn ways of preventing future accidents. You have been assigned to design a new accident report form which will help them achieve this goal.
Of the following, the item in the report that would be of MOST value to your safety experts for their purpose is 3._____

    A. the name and age of the accident victim
    B. a description of the working situation which led to the accident
    C. a statement from the foreman whether there was any carelessness involved
    D. a statement by the employee involved as to how the accident might have been prevented

4. A foreman should investigate every accident, including minor ones that do not involve injury, MAINLY because 4._____

    A. investigation of all accidents will help to increase the safety awareness of the employees
    B. each accident indicates a potential source of injury or damage
    C. the foreman will receive valuable experience in spotting hazardous conditions
    D. safety records should include all accidents regardless of seriousness

5. The following are methods used to prevent accidents. The one that is the MOST effective way to provide for safe and efficient operation of machines is to 5._____

    A. station guards on machines where physical hazards exist
    B. train employees in job procedures that will minimize accidents
    C. provide protective clothing and equipment for work on dangerous machines
    D. eliminate hazards by including safety considerations in the basic design

6. The MOST important element of preventive maintenance is

   A. calibration B. lubrication
   C. inspection   D. cleaning

7. Of the following statements, the one that is MOST accurate is that a supervisor is

   A. not responsible for power tools used by his men
   B. not responsible for power tools used by his men if the men are properly trained in the use of these power tools
   C. always responsible for power tools used by his men
   D. responsible for power tools used by his men only if there has not been adequate time to train the men in the use of the power tools

8. Assume that your crew has been issued an item of safety equipment and the men refuse to wear it because it is not the brand they are used to.
   You, as supervisor, should

   A. let them work without it until you check with your superior
   B. stop the men from working and report the facts to your superior immediately
   C. warn them that they may lose compensation payments if there is an accident
   D. have the supply man issue the proper equipment

9. A steel measuring tape is undesirable for use around electrical equipment.
   The LEAST important reason is the

   A. magnetic effect
   B. short circuit hazard
   C. shock hazard
   D. danger of entanglement in rotating machines

10. When using a portable extension cord, the MOST important precaution to take is to

    A. see that the cord does not create a tripping hazard
    B. make sure that the cord does not touch any metal
    C. have a polarized plug at the end of the cord
    D. keep the cord clean and dry

11. Of the following, the one which is MOST likely to have the GREATEST effect in improving safety is

    A. holding foremen accountable for accidents of subordinates
    B. periodic safety inspections
    C. posting numerous safety bulletins
    D. providing each worker with periodic safety newsletters

12. The proper extinguisher to use on an electrical fire in an operating electric motor is

    A. sand   B. water
    C. soda and acid D. carbon dioxide

13. When a container is used for flammable liquids, it usually presents the GREATEST hazard when it is   13.____

    A. empty but uncleaned   B. empty and clean
    C. filled   D. half-filled

14. Of the following cans, the SAFEST type of can to use for storing oil-soaked rags indoors is   14.____

    A. perforated sheet metal can with a sheet metal cover
    B. sheet metal can with a sheet metal cover
    C. sheet metal can without a cover
    D. sheet metal can with perforated sheet metal cover

15. To take the strain off the connections to an electrical plug, the knot which should be used is a(n)   15.____

    A. bowline   B. hitch
    C. underwriter's D. square

16. In analyzing safety performance, the term *injury frequency rate* is used. This is defined as the number of disabling injuries per 1,000,000 man-hours worked.   16.____
    If an assistant supervisor has 80 men under him working 40 hours a week and 5 men suffered disabling injuries in a working period of 52 weeks, then the injury frequency rate would be closest to

    A. 25   B. 30   C. 35   D. 40

17. Of the following, the organization that MOST often certifies to the safety of individual pieces of equipment is the   17.____

    A. American Society for Testing Materials
    B. Underwriters' Laboratories, Inc.
    C. American Standards Association
    D. Association of Casualty and Surety Companies

18. The extinguishing agent in a soda-acid fire extinguisher is   18.____

    A. water   B. carbon dioxide
    C. carbon tetrachloride D. calcium chloride solution

19. The proper technique for lifting heavy objects includes all of the following EXCEPT   19.____

    A. bending the knees
    B. placing the feet as far from the object as possible
    C. keeping the back straight
    D. lifting with the arras and legs

20. The one of the following methods which should NOT be used in treating portable wooden ladders is   20.____

    A. the application of a coat of clear lacquer
    B. thorough washing with soap and water
    C. the application of a coat of white paint
    D. the application of a coat of linseed oil

21. The MAIN reason for a requirement that defective material be removed from a job site as soon as possible is to

   A. prevent injuries
   B. reduce clutter in the area
   C. prevent accidental use of the material
   D. permit more efficient operation

21.____

22. The MAIN reason for reporting accidents is to

   A. prevent future accidents of the same type
   B. determine who was at fault
   C. prevent unwarranted lawsuits
   D. have a record of the causes of delays

22.____

23. Employees who must lift and carry stock items should be careful to avoid injury. When an employee lifts or carries stock items, which of the following is the LEAST safe practice?

   A. Keep the legs straight and lift with the back muscles
   B. Keep the load as close to the body as possible
   C. Get a good grip on the object to be carried
   D. First determine if the item can be lifted and carried safely

23.____

24. For warning and protection, the color *red* is usually for

   A. indicating high temperature stockroom areas
   B. floor markings
   C. location of first-aid supplies
   D. stop buttons, lights for barricades, and other dangerous locations

24.____

25. Reporting rattles, squeaks, or other noises in equipment to your maintenance supervisor is

   A. *bad;* too much attention to squeaks like these keep important safety problems from being noticed
   B. *bad;* each person should oil and care for his own equipment
   C. *good;* these sounds may mean that the equipment should be fixed
   D. *good;* it shows the supervisor that you are a good worker

25.____

KEY (CORRECT ANSWERS)

1.	B	11.	B
2.	A	12.	D
3.	B	13.	A
4.	B	14.	B
5.	D	15.	C
6.	C	16.	B
7.	C	17.	B
8.	B	18.	A
9.	A	19.	B
10.	A	20.	C

21. C
22. A
23. A
24. D
25. C

———

TEST 2

DIRECTIONS: Each question or incomplete statement is followed by several suggested answers or completions. Select the one that BEST answers the question or completes the statement. *PRINT THE LETTER OF THE CORRECT ANSWER IN THE SPACE AT THE RIGHT.*

1. An agency gives some of its maintenance employees instruction in first aid. The MOST likely reason for doing this is to

    A. eliminate the need for calling a doctor in case of accident
    B. reduce the number of accidents
    C. lower the cost of accidents to the agency
    D. provide temporary first aid

    1.____

2. If a fellow worker has stopped breathing after an electric shock, the BEST first-aid treatment is

    A. artificial respiration
    B. to massage his chest
    C. an application of cold compresses
    D. a hot drink

    2.____

3. If you had to telephone for an ambulance because of an accident, the MOST important information for you to give the person who answered the telephone would be the

    A. exact time of the accident
    B. place where the ambulance is needed
    C. cause of the accident
    D. names and addresses of those injured

    3.____

4. To use clean ice water as a treatment for burns is

    A. *good*, because it gives immediate relief from pain and seems to lessen the damaging effects of burns
    B. *bad*, because it has a tendency to cause frostbite which may develop into gangrene
    C. *good*, because ice water will destroy any bacteria at once
    D. *bad*, because the extremely cold temperature will cause a person to go into shock

    4.____

5. One of your men strained the muscles in his back when he attempted to lift a load that was extremely heavy.
   The treatment for this injury would include all of the following EXCEPT

    A. applying cold cloths or an ice bag to the back
    B. massaging the area
    C. resting the back in its most comfortable position
    D. rubbing the strained muscles with witch hazel

    5.____

6. A man who fainted in the terminal is now semiconscious. He is bleeding about the mouth and is in danger of choking on the blood.
   He should be placed on his

    6.____

- A. back, with his head slightly lower than his feet
- B. stomach, with his head turned to one side, lower than his feet
- C. back, with his feet slightly lower than his head
- D. stomach, with his head turned to one side, higher than his feet

7. When administering first aid to a helper suffering from shock as a result of falling off a high ladder, it is MOST important to

   - A. cover the helper and keep him warm
   - B. give the helper something to drink
   - C. apply artificial respiration to the helper
   - D. prop the helper up to a sitting position

8. If a co-worker's clothing gets caught in the gears of a machine in operation, the FIRST thing for a helper to do is to

   - A. call the supervisor
   - B. try to pull him out
   - C. shut off the machine's power
   - D. jam a metal tool between the gears of the machine

9. The one of the following which is the FIRST thing to do when a person gets an electric shock and is still in contact with the supply is to

   - A. start artificial respiration immediately
   - B. treat for burns
   - C. cut the power if it takes no more than 5 minutes to locate the switch
   - D. remove the victim from the contact by using a dry stick or dry rope

10. The one of the following that is the LEAST important health precaution for a worker to take is

    - A. frequent washing
    - B. shading his eyes from reflected light
    - C. using an antiseptic on cuts
    - D. wearing rubber gloves

11. Before entering a sewer which is known to contain dangerous gases, the able foreman will

    - A. drop lighted matches down the manhole
    - B. make sure all manholes in the vicinity are closed
    - C. send one man down to determine the amount of gas present
    - D. wait until the sewer has been ventilated

12. The one of the following that would MOST likely be the cause of a sewer explosion is

    - A. a pressure relief valve installed in the main sewer line
    - B. an unplugged opening left for a house connection
    - C. naphtha discharged into the sewer by a cleaning establishment
    - D. sewage of recent origin containing dissolved oxygen

13. In case of severe injury and where there is a possibility of broken bones, the MOST important precaution to take in giving first aid to an injured man is:

    A. Bundle him into an automobile and get him to a hospital as fast as possible
    B. Lower his feet and raise his head
    C. Move him no more than necessary and call a doctor
    D. Raise him to a sitting position and give him a drink of water

14. The logical reason that certain employees who work on the tracks carry small parts in fiber pails rather than steel pails is that fiber pails

    A. are stronger
    B. can't rust
    C. can't be dented by rough usage
    D. do not conduct electricity

15. While working on a certain track between stations, a helper notices a man standing on an adjacent track and suspects from the man's actions that he may have no business being there.
    The MOST reasonable procedure would be to

    A. continue working and ignore the man
    B. order the man to get off the tracks immediately
    C. ask the man what business he has being there
    D. hold the man for questioning by police

16. With respect to safety of personnel, it is probably LEAST important to

    A. have a place for each tool and put each tool in its place at the end of each day
    B. place each tool where it cannot fall down and hurt anyone when working on a job
    C. coat each tool with grease at the end of each day to prevent rust
    D. inspect carefully all tools to be used before beginning the day's work

17. Employees whose work requires them to enter upon the tracks are cautioned not to wear loose-fitting clothing. The MOST important reason for this caution is that loose-fitting clothing may

    A. interfere when they are using heavy tools
    B. catch on some projection of a passing train
    C. give insufficient protection against dust
    D. tear more easily than snug-fitting clothing

18. Recent safety reports indicate that a principal cause of injury to employees is *falls* while on a job. Such reports tend to emphasize that safety on the job is BEST assured by

    A. following every rule   B. keeping alert
    C. never working alone   D. working very slowly

19. The one of the following statements about a plug fuse that is MOST valid is that it should

    A. always be screwed in lightly to assure easy removal
    B. never be used to hold a coin in the fuse socket
    C. never be replaced by someone unfamiliar with the circuit
    D. always be replaced by a larger size if it burns out frequently

20. If a helper has frequent accidents, it is MOST likely that he is   20._____

    A. not physically strong enough to do the job
    B. simply one of those persons who is unlucky
    C. not paying enough attention to safe work habits
    D. trying too hard

21. A rule states that, *In walking on the track, walk opposite to the direction of traffic on that*   21._____
    track if possible.
    By logical reasoning, the PRINCIPAL safety idea behind this rule is that the man on the track

    A. is more likely to see an approaching train
    B. will be seen more readily by the motorman
    C. need not be as careful
    D. is better able to judge the speed of the train

22. The PRINCIPAL objection to using water from a hose to put out a fire involving live electrical equipment is that   22._____

    A. insulation may be damaged
    B. cast iron parts may rust
    C. serious electric shock may result
    D. a short-circuit will result

23. An electrician's knife should NOT be used to   23._____

    A. cut copper wires   B. remove rubber insulation
    C. cut friction tape   D. sharpen pencils

24. According to a safety report, a frequent cause of accidents to workers is the improper use of tools.   24._____
    The MOST helpful conclusion that you can draw from this statement is that

    A. most tools are difficult to use properly
    B. most tools are dangerous to use
    C. many accidents from tools are unavoidable
    D. many accidents from tools occur because of poor working habits

25. When a maintainer reports a minor trouble orally to his foreman, the MOST important   25._____
    information the foreman would require from the maintainer would be the

    A. type of trouble and its exact location
    B. names of all men with him when he discovered the trouble
    C. exact time the trouble was discovered
    D. work he was doing when he noted the trouble

KEY (CORRECT ANSWERS)

1. D
2. A
3. B
4. A
5. A

6. B
7. A
8. C
9. D
10. B

11. D
12. C
13. C
14. D
15. C

16. C
17. B
18. B
19. B
20. C

21. A
22. C
23. A
24. D
25. A

EXAMINATION SECTION
TEST 1

DIRECTIONS: Each question or incomplete statement is followed by several suggested answers or completions. Select the one that BEST answers the question or completes the statement. *PRINT THE LETTER OF THE CORRECT ANSWER IN THE SPACE AT THE RIGHT.*

1. One of your subordinates, whom you consider to be a troublemaker because of his poor attitude toward his work, has been complaining to other employees about his work and stirring them up to make similar complaints. For you to respond to his actions discreetly and impersonally without any show of emotion or upset is considered to be

   A. *good* practice; you may change his attitudes for the better
   B. *good* practice; he may be so frustrated by your reaction that he will request a transfer
   C. *poor* practice; other employees may follow his example and choose him as their spokesman
   D. *poor* practice; he may not know how to respond to your lack of emotion

2. The practice of a foreman's requesting his subordinates to submit suggestions regarding ways of reducing costs is

   A. *inadvisable;* reducing costs is the foreman's responsibility, not that of his subordinates
   B. *inadvisable* he may waste a great deal of time by having to review worthless suggestions
   C. *advisable;* it will give subordinates something to do when they have no work to occupy them
   D. *advisable;* asking subordinates for ideas on cost reduction will make them feel more involved in the work process

3. Of the following, which is the BEST way to store steel pipe and other similarly shaped metal pieces?

   A. Stack in layers, with alternating rows of materials placed lengthwise and widthwise
   B. Stack in a pyramid shape, with sheets of wood placed between the layers
   C. Stack in layers, with strips of iron, the ends of which are turned up, placed between the layers
   D. In vertical rows, upright against a wall

4. Which one of the following is NOT a usual hazard of handling and servicing storage batteries?

   A. Acid burns
   B. Bruised knuckles
   C. Lead poisoning
   D. Electric shock

5. As a foreman, at which point should you report an employee to your superior for working in an unsafe manner?

   A. The first time he does something that endangers himself or another employee
   B. Usually not at all; this is a matter that should be handled by the foreman
   C. When you become aware of a pattern of unsafe operations in his work
   D. When an accident occurs

6. In order to prevent a fire, oily work rags should be

   A. kept in covered metal containers
   B. kept in neat piles in a well-ventilated area
   C. kept in open storage boxes, at least ten feet away from any flammable material
   D. wrapped in newspaper and stacked neatly against a fireproof wall

7. For which one of the following uses would it be UNSAFE to use a carpenter's hammer? Striking a

   A. casing nail   B. hand punch
   C. hardened steel surface D. plastic surface

8. When a certain gasoline tank is filled to capacity, it holds 420 gallons. If it is 3/4 full, the number of gallons of gasoline it is holding is

   A. 280   B. 315   C. 360   D. 375

9. Eight men working full time take 16 days to do a job. How long should it take if four men do this job? _____ days.

   A. 26   B. 28   C. 32   D. 38

10. If 20 feet of lumber costs $62.00, the cost of 45 feet would be

    A. $136.25   B. $139.50   C. $144.25   D. $149.50

11.

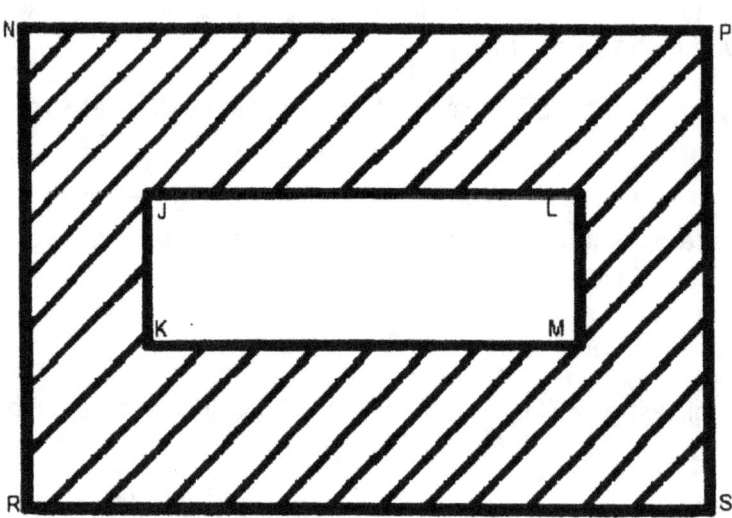

Shown above is a rectangle (JKLM) inside another rectangle (NPSR). What is the area of the shaded portion if LM measures 20 feet, JL measures 30 feet, NR measures 45 feet, and RS measures 55 feet?
_____ square feet.

   A. 600   B. 975   C. 1,875   D. 2,475

12. To produce a certain cleaning compound, four materials, W, X, Y, and Z, are combined by mixing 6 pounds of W, 5 pounds of X, 3 pounds of Y, and 1 pound of Z.
    In order to make up 270 pounds of this cleaning compound, the number of pounds of W required is _____ pounds.

    A. 100   B. 108   C. 112   D. 120

13. The normal work week for a laborer is 35 hours.
    If a laborer spends 27 hours at Job Location A and the rest of his work week at Job Location B, the percentage of time spent at Job Location B is MOST NEARLY _____ percent.

    A. 19   B. 21   C. 23   D. 25

14. Which one of the following is the GENERALLY recommended method of assigning work to your subordinates?

    A. Jobs are given to each man according to his ability to perform the job.
    B. Jobs that take the shortest time are given to the workers with the greatest seniority.
    C. The same amount of work is distributed to each man all of the time.
    D. Least important jobs are given to the less experienced workers.

15. Which one of the following tasks USUALLY requires two men to work together until the task is completed?

    A. Removing glass partitions from one location and reinstalling them in another
    B. Repairing a leaking faucet
    C. Filling requisitions from stock bins
    D. Clearing walkways of ice and snow

Questions 16–17.

DIRECTIONS: Questions 16 and 17 are to be answered on the basis of the following report.

To: Al Forbes   Date: March 30
      Director, Building Maintenance
                                              Subject:
From: Jim Harris
      Foreman

On March 30, at 10:30 A.M., while working on a piece of sheet metal in the machine shop, Steve Farrell cut his hand so badly that he was rushed to the hospital and required 10 stitches. After the accident, it was determined that Steve had not been wearing gloves when the accident occurred. It is, therefore, suggested that safety procedures for materials handling be reviewed so that an accident such as this may be prevented in the future.

16. The subject of the report has been left out.
    Which of the following would be BEST as the subject of this report?

    A. Dangerous Conditions in the Machine Shop
    B. Carelessness of Employees Working in the Machine Shop
    C. Procedures for Handling Accidents
    D. Report of Accident Due to Unsafe Materials Handling

17. Of the following, this report is unsatisfactory because it omits   17._____

    A. a recommendation for disciplinary action against Steve Farrell
    B. details regarding how the accident occurred
    C. Steve Farrell's prior accident record
    D. the number of sick days that Steve Farrell has available

18. Suppose an employee under your supervision appears to be developing the habit of   18._____
    wandering off for a half-hour or more almost every afternoon without offering any
    explanation.
    The FIRST thing you should do in this situation is to

    A. assign extra work to the employee so that he will have no time to wander off
    B. reprimand the employee officially and give him a copy of the reprimand
    C. transfer the employee to another type of work and observe if his behavior remains
       the same
    D. talk to the employee about the reasons why he is leaving the job site

19. Of the following, the MAIN advantage of having one employee responsible for the issu-   19._____
    ance of tools is

    A. it assures that the right tool will be used for a particular job
    B. tools will be less likely to be damaged
    C. it insures accountability for the tools
    D. it discourages the use of an employee's personal tools

20. After being inspected, a new ladder is usually coated with a preservative such as clear   20._____
    varnish.
    Of the following, the MAIN reason for using a clear preservative is that

    A. the name of the department imprinted on the ladder can be easily identified
    B. defects occurring after the inspection can be easily noticed
    C. workers using the ladder are likely to maintain a new ladder in good condition
    D. cracks in the ladder are less likely to occur than if the ladder were painted

KEY (CORRECT ANSWERS)

1. A
2. D
3. C
4. C
5. C

6. A
7. C
8. B
9. C
10. B

11. C
12. B
13. C
14. A
15. A

16. D
17. B
18. D
19. C
20. B

TEST 2

DIRECTIONS: Each question or incomplete statement is followed by several suggested answers or completions. Select the one that BEST answers the question or completes the statement. *PRINT THE LETTER OF THE CORRECT ANSWER IN THE SPACE AT THE RIGHT.*

1. Assume that you, a foreman, expect that some of your workers will have an objection to an order that you must issue.
   If it is not an emergency order, it is MOST advisable for you to

   A. explain to your workers that you do not agree with the order, but that you have no power to do anything but follow it
   B. issue the order without comment and discourage discussion or objections by your workers
   C. state and explain the order carefully to your workers and allow them time to ask questions and to discuss with you their objections
   D. warn your workers before issuing the order that you will take disciplinary action against anyone who resists carrying out the order

   1.____

2. On the job, practical jokes have been played frequently upon one particular man under your supervision. When you, as a foreman, ask the reason for such behavior by the men who play these tricks, they say they do this because the victim invites these tricks upon himself.
   Of the following, it is MOST appropriate for you, the foreman, to FIRST

   A. warn each man involved in such acts that these practical jokes must be discontinued immediately
   B. post a written notice addressed to all the men under your supervision warning them of the dangers involved in playing practical jokes
   C. review the work schedule of your subordinates to see that they have enough work to occupy them for a full day
   D. ask the man on whom the tricks were played if he resents being the victim of such tricks

   2.____

3. Under which one of the following circumstances would it be BEST for a foreman to give orders in the form of commands rather than requests?
   When a foreman

   A. is giving orders to one employee directly rather than to the entire crew
   B. is giving orders that require additional instructions as the work progresses
   C. is giving orders to his entire crew to cope with a critical situation
   D. has been ordered by his supervisor to furnish a skeleton crew for holiday work

   3.____

4. When carrying objects on a two-wheeled handtruck, placing the heavier objects on the bottom of the load is a

   A. *good* practice, because the lighter objects are less likely to be damaged
   B. *poor* practice, because the lighter objects are more likely to fall off
   C. *good* practice, because more weight can be loaded on the truck
   D. *poor* practice, because it will be harder to start the truck in motion

   4.____

5. Of the following, the MAIN advantage in using a Phillips head screw is that

   A. the threads of the Phillips head screw have a deeper bite than standard screw threads
   B. the screwdriver used on this type of screw is more likely to keep its edge than a standard screwdriver
   C. a single screwdriver fits all size screws of this type
   D. the screwdriver used on this type of screw is less likely to slip than a standard screwdriver

6. One of the reasons why a polyester rope is considered to be the BEST general-purpose rope is that it _____ ropes made of other materials.

   A. does not stretch as much as
   B. is available in longer lengths than
   C. does not fray as much as
   D. contains more strands than

7. A daily inspection tour by the foreman would be of GREATEST benefit to him and his subordinates when the subordinates realize that the foreman

   A. is available to answer any questions they might have about the work
   B. is checking up on them to make certain they are not wasting time
   C. is looking for the type of work that will bring his name to the attention of his superiors
   D. will lend a hand to get the daily work accomplished

8. For you to use different methods of discipline for each employee is considered to be

   A. *good* practice; each employee should be disciplined in a manner that is most effective for him
   B. *good* practice; your employees will be afraid to misbehave because they can no longer predict your behavior
   C. *poor* practice, employees may consider these different methods a sign of indecisiveness and lose respect for you
   D. *poor* practice; an employee who believes he is getting the harshest discipline may become hostile and antagonistic

9. As a foreman, you have just informed your crew that you want them to follow a new procedure when signing out for tools from the tool cabinet.
   Of the following, the MOST efficient method for you to adopt to make certain that your crew is reminded of this new procedure is to

   A. take each man aside and tell him you are counting on him to follow the correct procedure
   B. announce to the men that all tools in the cabinet are stamped with a serial number and the agency name
   C. post instructions for the new procedure at the tool cabinet so the men will be sure to see then when requisitioning tools
   D. question the men at their work sites to learn whether they obtained the tools by following the new procedure

10. For you as a foreman to tell an individual employee how much he is expected to do on a job assignment is a

    A. *good* practice, because he will have a goal to try to reach
    B. *bad* practice, because he will be able to determine if you are giving others the same amount of work
    C. *good* practice, because you will be able to give the individual more detailed instructions on how to do the job
    D. *bad* practice, because he will do the minimum amount of work and not be motivated to continue further

11. A laborer who has worked in your agency for five years has just been transferred into your unit.
    In order for you to be able to plan his assignments properly, the FIRST thing you should do is to

    A. ask him what he already knows about the work handled in your unit
    B. plan a training program for him in which all phases of your unit's operations are covered
    C. assign one of your more experienced laborers to train him in the work of your unit
    D. tell him what you want him to do and then interview him

12. After you have assigned a job to one of your workers, he complains to your superior about the job instead of coming to you with his complaint. He recognizes that it is proper to discuss the complaint with you first. However, he points out that in the past other employees under your supervision have successfully bypassed you with their complaints. Which of the following approaches generally would be MOST productive in getting your subordinates to turn to you first with their complaints?

    A. Ask your superior how he handled this complaint, so that you can handle it in the same way when the complaint arises again.
    B. Clarify the steps of the complaint procedure with your employees.
    C. Ask your superior to take no action on the employee complaints, but to refer the employee to you, their supervisor.
    D. Tell your employees that if they do not bring the complaints to you first, they cannot take them to your superior.

13. Of the following, the MAIN reason that on-the-job training is widely used is that

    A. the trainee can be producing while he is being trained
    B. the supervisor can assign several trainees to the training at one time
    C. the trainee can progress at his own speed
    D. most supervisors are well-qualified to conduct on-the-job training

14. Of the following, it is BEST for a foreman to begin a new employee's training right after the new employee has

    A. made several errors in performing the first task he has been given to do
    B. had an opportunity to meet all the other employees having his title
    C. reported for work in the unit
    D. shown an interest in learning more about the job he has been doing

15. As a foreman, you have always handwritten accident reports. However, a new accident reporting procedure requests that you use a printed form which asks specific questions and provides blank spaces where the information about the accident can be filled in.
    Of the following, the MOST important advantage of using this printed form is that

    A. the information can be completed by any one of your workers if you are not available
    B. your supervisor can rely on information in a printed form to be more reliable than a completely handwritten report
    C. you can enter as much or as little information on the form as you think necessary
    D. you will be less likely to omit needed information

16. If you replace a blown fuse, and the replaced fuse has burned out shortly thereafter, the FIRST step that should be taken when the replaced fuse has been damaged is that

    A. this second fuse should be replaced by a new fuse of the same type and amperage
    B. this second fuse should be replaced by a new fuse of slightly greater amperage
    C. the circuit should be disconnected while the cause of the burn-out is determined
    D. a check of all other fuses at the electrical connection should be made to determine if they were in working order

17. When you are placing a 12-foot portable ladder with a non-slip base against the side of a building, the distance from the base of the ladder to the base of the side of the building should be MOST NEARLY, according to general safety rules, _____ feet.

    A. 2   B. 3   C. 4   D. 6

18. A foreman must supply sufficient plywood paneling, each panel measuring 4 feet by 8 feet, to erect a three-sided barrier fence 8 feet high in front of a building entrance. This rectangular area will be closed to the public while the building alterations are made. The longer side of the area measures 24 feet, and each of the shorter sides measures 12 feet.
    The MINIMUM number of plywood panels necessary to erect this fence is

    A. 9   B. 12   C. 18   D. 24

19. The proper saw to use to cut wood with the grain is a _____ saw.

    A. hack   B. crosscut   C. back   D. rip

20. One of your men, Tom Jones, has shown up late for work several times in the past two weeks. The quality of his work, however, is good. This morning, Jones comes in late again.
Of the following, the FIRST action you should take is to

    A. warn Jones that if his lateness continues he will be disciplined
    B. send Jones to the Personnel Officer for disciplinary action
    C. speak to your own supervisor and ask him what to do in this case
    D. ask Jones why he has been arriving late for work so often lately

20.____

KEY (CORRECT ANSWERS)

1.	C	11.	A
2.	A	12.	C
3.	C	13.	A
4.	A	14.	C
5.	D	15.	D
6.	A	16.	C
7.	A	17.	B
8.	A	18.	B
9.	C	19.	D
10.	A	20.	D

PIPEFITTING

The term "pipe fitting" includes the operations which must be performed in installing a pipe system as made up of pipe and fittings. These operations consist of:

1. Pipe cutting
2. Pipe threading
3. Pipe tapping
4. Pipe bending
5. Assembling

The mechanic who performs the work of pipe fitting is called a *pipe fitter*, and sometimes a *steam fitter*, because the work is largely connected with steam installations. Considerable experience is necessary to become a good pipe fitter, and there are a good many persons engaged in this occupation who do not deserve the title of steam fitter.

Pipe Cutting

Wrought pipe as received from the manufacturers, comes in lengths varying from 12 to 22 feet, and in "pipe fitting" it is frequently necessary to cut it to any particular length that may be required. This may be done with a hacksaw or a pipe cutter, the pipe in either case being put in a pipe vise.

In securing the pipe in the vise, care should be taken (especially when threading, that the jaws hold the pipe sufficiently firmly to prevent slipping, but the clamp screw should not be turned enough to cause the jaw teeth to unduly dig into the pipe.

A pipe cutter may be defined as an instrument usually consisting of a hook-shaped frame on whose stem a slide can be moved by a screw. On the slide and frame several cutting discs or "wheels" are mounted and forced into the metal as the whole appliance is rotated about the pipe.

Pipe cutters may be classed as:
1. Wheel
2. Combined roller and wheel
3. Knife

The operation of cutting a pipe can be done quicker with a pipe cutter than a hacksaw, and for this reason the former is more frequently used, although it crushes the metal and leaves a shoulder on the outside and a burr on the inside of the pipe. This does not apply to the knife type of pipe cutter.

The external shoulder must be removed to allow the pipe to enter the threading tool so no worry need be given that the workman will not do this, but it should be ascertained by inspection that the internal burr is removed on every cut, especially on plumbing jobs, to avoid future trouble with clogged pipes.

There are two types of wheel cutter. The one-wheel cutter is adapted more for shop use than for general work. The three-wheel cutter is the best type cutter on the market for general work. With this cutter, the work of cutting is distributed among the three wheels, whereas with the one-wheel cutter, one wheel has to do all the work.

Although the rollers insure a straight cut, a little care in starting a three-wheel cutter is all that is necessary to obtain a straight cut; moreover, the range of work possible with a three-wheel cutter is greater than that with a one-wheel or combined roller and wheel cutter. When the wheels become dull or nicked, they are easily removed and renewed at nominal expense.

The knife cutter makes a clear cut like a hacksaw but is a more expensive tool than the other types.

Too much attention cannot be given to removing burrs produced by wheel cutters because the burr usually has a ragged and sharp edge, which catches any sediment or other foreign matter passing through the pipe and finally stops the flow. The proper and convenient way to remove a burr is by a brace and burring reamer.

Pipe Threading

Having cut the pipe to proper length, filed off the outer shoulder and reamed out the burr, it is now ready for the threading operation. The Briggs threads may be cut on the pipe ends for screwing into the fittings either by means of

1. Hand stock and dies, or
2. Pipe threading machines.

The hand stock and dies being portable are generally used for small jobs, especially for threading pipe of the smaller size, although there are some geared forms suitable for large work without undue physical effort; the threading machines are for use in shops where a large amount of threading is done. Hand stock and dies may be classed with respect to the dies, as

1. Solid
2. Sectional
3. Adjustable
4. Expanding
5. Receding

In use, the dies are placed in these types and are adjusted to the variations in the size of fittings by the set screws at the ends and secured by the bolts which pass through the dies, the holes in the dies being sufficiently larger than the bolts to allow the necessary lateral adjustment movement.

The term *expanding* is used to represent that class of threads in which one set of dies is used for all sizes of pipe having the same number of threads, the dies being moved closer or farther apart by means of cams or equivalent. Since only five different thread pitches are used in the entire range of pipe sizes, the advantage of this in adapting a stock for quick change is apparent.

The *receding* form of threader employs tapered posts or levers against which the back ends of the dies rest. In cutting a thread, the dies at the beginning of the operation cut a full depth thread. As the work progresses (taking the lever type for illustration), the levers which support the dies gradually change their position, permitting the dies to *recede* until they have finally backed completely away from the pipe. The stock can then be pulled straight off the pipe, thus avoiding unwinding or backing off.

The proper method of cutting a thread with stock and dies: Use plenty of oil in starting and cutting the thread. In starting, press the dies firmly against the pipe end until they "take hold." After a few turns, blow out the chips and apply more oil. This should be done two or three times before completing the cut. When complete, blow out chips as clean as possible and back off the die. Avoid the frequent reversal usually made by some pipe fitters.

For lubrication, lard will be found preferable to oil. Apply the lard to the pipe end with a brush. In cutting the thread, the heat generated will melt the lard which will flow to the cutting edge of the die giving continuous lubrication instead of spasmodic flooding as is the case when using oil.

Flat Threads

A considerable amount of material is discarded on account of the threads being a trifle flat, and such practice may be regarded as due to ignorance.

Occasionally pipe is rejected on account of small grooves that sometimes occur in threads because the weld is not perfectly brought up.

A groove of this kind could not possibly produce a leak unless it ran the entire length of the thread contact, and in depth went below the bottom of the thread; such defect is, however, rarely encountered.

Making Tight Joints For Very High Pressures

There are many pipe fitters who do not understand the conditions that are necessary in order to make good screw joints with pipe and fittings, especially when they are intended to withstand very high pressure. Tight joints for 1,000 lbs. air may be made with the ordinary line pipe, providing clean cut threads are made, and extraordinary care and intelligence is exercised in putting them together. The secret of making a tight joint is to avoid or overcome the friction incident to screwing pipe and fittings together.

The importance of avoiding friction and heat is illustrated in one instance where a pipe line was being put together in the field by machinery. The machine would do the work quickly, and the workmen concluded that they had tight joints, when the joints became hot; but after the material was cold, and the heat of the friction was gone, the joints would not be tight. The fact of the matter was that the heat showed conclusively that the threads had not been properly cleaned, and instead of the heat being an evidence of a tight joint, it was evidence of a bad joint.

It must be evident to anyone who has given any thought whatever to this subject that in order to make good joints, the iron must be brought together as solidly as possible. To secure this result, the first essential is that the threads should be absolutely clean; and the next is that the very best lubricant should be used in order to prevent friction, and they should not be screwed up fast enough to make any change in the temperature of the material.

It is necessary that the threads be cut clean, that is, that taps and dies be in perfect condition.

A taper thread is not absolutely necessary to the making of a tight joint. (In one experiment, The Crane Co. made one joint with coupling which had no taper at all, and the others but very little.) Nor is a large amount of bearing necessary to make a tight joint – although for permanency and serviceability the standard length of threads and taper is considered necessary and correct.

It must be evident that the longer the thread the more tendency to friction, which prevents the iron coming up close together, not to mention the natural irregularities in the threads acting in the same direction. It should be understood that absence of heat in pipe or coupling does not mean absence of grit or gum in the threads. Dirty threads may be screwed up very slowly, and thus avoid the heating due to friction, and yet the joint be anything but tight.

Cutting Nipples

The pipe fitting usually makes any nipples required, but usually better nipples (especially the close and short variety) can be obtained from the supply house at less cost.

No pipe fitter deserving to be called such will attempt to cut nipples without a proper nipple holder, although some plumbers and others are often guilty of such practice when working by the day instead of by the job.

The ordinary method of cutting nipples, as indulged in by some plumbers and others, for lack of proper tools, is very unsatisfactory.

This consists of using a short piece of pipe with a coupling on the end as a homemade nipple holder. This is placed in the pipe vise and a piece of pipe threaded on one end screwed tightly with the coupling, and after cutting off to length desired for the nipple, an attempt is made to thread the other end. Owing to the considerable effort required to cut the thread, the nipple turns in the coupling until the latter is strained to the splitting point and in fact usually does split before many nipples have been cut in this way, resulting in profanity and a waste of time.

In emergency, the proper way to cut a nipple with such makeshift holder so as not to split the coupling is to use adjustable dies, as, for instance, the Armstrong pattern. First take a very light cut, then adjust dies and take one or more additional cuts to finish. The cost of a properly made nipple holder is so small that it should be included in very pipe threading outfit.

Calculation of Offsets

In pipe fitting, the term *offset* may be defined as *a change of direction (other than 90°) in a pipe bringing one part out of, but parallel with the line of another.*

Pipe Tapping

Frequently in pipe fitting, it is necessary to cut internal threads on pipes, as in making pipe headers, lubricator connections, etc. This is called *tapping*, and involves (1) drilling holes to correct diameter, (2) sometimes reaming, and (3) cutting the internal threads by means of a *tap*. It is first necessary to know what size hole is required for the size of tap.

In drilling a pipe for tapping, care should be taken that the drill be guided in a radial direction and perpendicular to the pipe axis.

Pipe Bending

There are numerous instances where it is desirable to bend the pipe rather than use additional fittings to make directional changes in the pipe line. With the proper facilities, pipe may be bent within certain limits without difficulty.

Assembling

On large jobs the pipe is usually cut according to a sketch or working drawing and partly assembled at the shop. If no mistakes have been made in following the dimensions on the drawing, and the latter be correct, the pipe and fittings may be installed without difficulty, that is, the last joint will come together or "make up". This last joint is either a union, a right and left, or long screw joint, and if errors have been made in cutting the pipe, it will be difficult or impossible to make up this closing joint.

On small jobs, no sketch is necessary, the fitter proportioning the pipe lengths mostly "by eye," taking occasional measurements where necessary during the progress of the work. It should be noted that with the great variety of fittings available, any pipe system may be arranged in numerous ways and the proper selection of these fittings and general arrangement of the system so that it will be direct, simple, accessible for repairs, etc., is an index of the fitter's ability.

In making up screwed joints, red or white lead, graphite, or some standard joint cement should be used. Of these, red lead is most extensively used. It is no doubt most efficient in making a tight joint, but it is more difficult to unscrew the fitting in case of repairs than when graphite is used.

Size of Steam Pipes

This is governed by the velocity of steam within them and by the radiation. As the size decreases, the steam velocity and the pressure drop for a given quantity naturally increases; on the other hand, the larger the pipe, the greater the radiation and the greater the amount of condensation; hence, the designer has to intelligently consider these opposing effects. In practice, the limiting factor in the velocity advisable is the allowable pressure drop between the boiler and the engine.

Strength of Pipes

Careful judgment must be exercised by the designer in determining the strength or weight of pipes to be used and sufficient allowances made for the pressure and temperature, size of mains and branches, expansion and contraction, water hammer, vibration, settling, and corrosion.

Since the effects of the disturbing influences can only be assumed, a high factor of safety should be employed. For steam mains, it should never be less than 6, even under the most favorable conditions; and where the stresses due to the various forces are likely to be severe, a factor as high as 15 may be employed to advantage.

Condensation and Water Hammer

With the proper size and strength of pipe determined, the most important factor is the prevention of water pockets and the removal of water condensation that will occur in any system. Water is practically incompressible, and its action when traveling at high velocities differs little from that of a solid body of equal weight, hence impact against elbows, valves or other obstructions is the equivalent of a heavy hammer blow that may result in a disastrous fracture of the fitting or pipe.

To avoid water hammer, the installation of efficient means for removing condensate is imperative, and the following suggestions as to such means may be of service:

1. The pitch of all pipes should be in the direction of the flow of steam.
2. Wherever a rise is necessary, a drain should be installed.
3. Main headers and important branches should end in a drop leg, each of which should be connected to the drainage system.
4. All low points in the piping should be drained and a drainage connection should be made to every fitting where there is danger of a water pocket.
5. Branch lines should, where possible, be taken from the top of a main header, but never from the bottom.
6. Valves should be so located that they cannot form water pockets when either open or closed. For this reason, globe valves should be set within the stem horizontal.
7. Where valves are placed directly on the boiler nozzle, a drain should be provided at the lowest point above the valve seat.
8. When two valves are installed between a boiler and the main header, a drain should be installed between them.

Steam Pipe Coverings

When steam pipes are exposed to the air, the steam condenses more or less rapidly, according to the temperature and circulation of the air surrounding them, causing a serious loss not only in the volume of steam, but of efficiency in utilizing the remainder when it reaches the engine. To reduce this loss, steam pipes, heaters, separators, valves, fittings, etc. should be effectively covered with a good heating-insulating material. An efficient covering should not deteriorate seriously from the heat or vibration to which it is subjected, and in all cases where it is necessary to consider the fire risk, should be made of non-combustible substances.

All surfaces to be covered should be painted before the material is applied. To insure lasting economy, pipe coverings must receive the same care and frequent inspection as any other part of a steam plant. Their efficiency quickly falls off if air be permitted to circulate between them and the pipe, and if allowed to become wet they only increase the evil they are expected to remedy.

Expansion and Support of Pipes

In arranging steam or hot water pipes, the greatest care must be taken, particularly with the former, to provide for the variations in length and form, due to temperature changes, without allowing the pipes and fittings to be subjected to undue strains. At certain points the pipes should be securely anchored, and at other places supports of the sliding type or flexible hangers must be provided. Expansion of the pipes is taken care of by such a method of support and by the provision of large radius bends or expansion joints where necessary.

If the expansion and contraction of steam pipes is not adequately provided for, stresses sufficient to cause permanent distortion of valve bodies will be thrown upon them, to the utter ruination of their finely machined or ground seat bearings, and likewise joint leaks will be much more prevalent and serious then when conditions are normal.

Alignment and Vibration

While these and other elements involving constructive details are generally understood and provided for in practice, there are instances where they are not given the attention they should receive, to the detriment of valves, fittings, and joints in the piping system. Correct alignment involves careful workmanship in the preparation and erection of the various units, to the end that they match up properly without pulling them together by means of unions or flange bolts. Vibration tendencies are controlled by suitable supports and braces which will prevent lateral movements and at the same time allow the pipe sufficient freedom for lengthwise expansion and contraction.

Corrosion

In the treatment of this element, special consideration must be given to local conditions. In all cases where iron or steel pipes are exposed to moist air, they should be protected by impervious and durable coatings. Likewise, as noted under *Steam Pipe Coverings*, all surfaces to be insulated should be similarly protected.

Internal corrosion is caused by solvent or oxidizing properties of water accelerated by the salts and gases dissolved in it and by the presence of air. Hence, the necessity of purifying the feed water of these harmful agents before using it in a boiler. To this end, the safest plan is to consult a competent chemist experienced in the analysis and treatment of boiler feed water and follow his recommendations.

Valve Connections

The use of screw or flange connections on valves and fittings is a question of individual judgment or preference, based upon working conditions and structural considerations. A good general rule for valves is to use flanges on sizes 2½ inches and larger for high steam pressures, 4 inches and larger for medium pressures, and 6 inches and larger for exhaust lines; smaller sizes may have screw connections.

Calculation of Pipe Sizes

To efficiently convey steam or water through a pipe under pressure, the pipe must not be too small or there will be an undue drop in pressure, nor too large, in the case of a steam pipe, because of the increased condensation.

SOIL PIPE FITTINGS

Quality of Iron

The iron composing the pipe and fittings must be of such composition and the condition of manufacture so maintained that the resulting pipe and fittings are of a compact, close-grained metal and are not hard, brittle, nor difficult to cut with file or chisel.

The constituents of the iron must be so regulated by utilizing raw material of known chemical composition and by calculating the chemical constituents of the charges daily that the iron maintains uniform physical characteristics.

Weights

In general, the weights and measurements of pipe and fittings shall be taken as those of plain uncoated pipe. All weights are in pounds.

Tests of Material

From each heat at intervals of not more than four hours' operation, there shall be made three bars, test being based on the average results of these three bars.

The bars, when placed flat-wise upon supports 24" apart and loaded in the center, shall support a load of not less than 2,000 lbs. and show a deflection of not less than 0.30" before breaking, or if preferred, tensile bars shall be made which will show a breaking point of not less than 20,000 lbs. per sq. in.

Testing of Pipe and Fittings

All pipe and fittings must be tested to a hydrostatic pressure of not less than 50 pounds to the square inch before coating. Any casting showing defects under this hydrostatic test shall be promptly broken and returned to the cupola.

Coating

Where pipe or fittings are to be coated, the method employed must be as follows: The coating shall be of coal tar pitch varnish. The varnish shall be made from coal tar. This material must contain sufficient oil to make a smooth coating, tough and tenacious when cold, and not brittle nor having any tendency to scale off.

Each casting shall be heated to a temperature of 300 degrees F immediately before it is dipped and shall possess not less than this temperature at the time it is put in the bath. The pipe and fittings must be uniformly heated so that the coating throughout has the proper qualities.

Each casting shall remain in the bath at least two minutes. The varnish shall be heated to 300 degrees F and shall remain at this temperature during the time the casting is immersed.

Fresh pitch and oil shall be added when necessary to keep the mixture at the proper consistency, and the vat shall be emptied of its contents and refilled with fresh pitch whenever the accumulation of sand or carbonaceous matter renders this desirable, as can be seen by the adhering solids to the underside or lower ends of the castings. After being coated, the pipe and fittings shall be carefully drained of the surplus varnish.

Inspection

All pipe and fittings must be carefully examined for defects, and sounded with a hammer before shipment. No filling with metal, cement or other material or so-called burning on of iron is to be permitted. The castings must be sound and free from cracks, sand holes, blow holes, and cold shots.

Inside Diameter

The inside diameter of the barrel of any pipe or fittings or branch thereof shall not be less at any point than $1/8$" less than the nominal size of same.

Outside Diameter

The outside diameter of the barrel of pipe and fittings shall be ½" greater than its nominal inside diameter. A variation in the outside diameter of $1/8$" above or below these figures will be permitted.

Wall Thickness

All pipe and fittings must be of uniform wall thickness and must present at the hub and spigot ends a true circle. A variation of $1/16$" less than the figures below will be permitted, but only when the actual weight is not less than the variation of the marked or estimated weight as set forth:

WALL THICKNESS

Barrel	Body of Hub	Through Bead of Hub	Through Bead at Spigot End
¼"	$5/16$"	½"	$7/16$"

The wall of all pipe and fittings must be smooth and free from fins and ridges which restrict the full effective area. All pipe must be thoroughly milled and free from adhering sand.

Hubs

The depth of hub shall be the distance, measured parallel to the axis of the opening, from the end of the hub to the beginning of any offset or change of direction of the inside wall of same. The depth of hubs shall not be less than as follows:

| Size of Pipe | 2" | 3" | 4" to 6" |
| Depth of Hub | 2¼" | 2½" | 2¾" |

The spigot end shall telescope not less than as follows:

2"	3"	4" to 6"
2½"	2¾"	3"

Hub bead shall have at its greatest diameter a width as follows:

2"	3"	4" to 6"
5/8"	11/16"	¾"

The inside diameter of the hubs shall be:

2"	3"	4"	5"	6"
3 3/16"	4 3/16"	5 3/16"	6 3/16"	7 3/16"

A variation in these diameters of 1/16" will be permitted.

Spigots

The outside diameter of the spigot bead must be 2 7/8" on 2"; 3 7/8" on 3"; 4 7/8" on 4", 5 7/8" on 5"; and 6 7/8" on 6". A variation in these diameters of 1/16" will be permitted.

Caulking Room

The spigot end, including bead, of every fitting must be straight without offset or change in direction for at least 4", except that on 3" bends this may be 3½", and on 2" bends, 3"; on all traps this must be at least 5". The laying length of a fitting is the overall length less the telescoping.

Radius of Fittings

The standard radii for bends, offsets, and traps are:

BENDS

	Size				
All Degrees	2"	3"	4"	5"	6"
Radius, Regular	3"	3½"	4"	4½"	5"
Radius, Short Sweep	5"	5½"	6"	6½"	7"
Radius, Long Sweep	8"	8½"	9"	9½"	10"

The given radii of regular bends are the same as those for sanitary T's, combination Y and 1/8 bends, upright Y's and vent branches. Bends radii shall be to center line of fitting.

Offsets

The radii of the bends on offsets, both regular and 1/8 bend offsets, shall be as follows:

Diameter	2"	3"	4"	5"	6"
Radius	2"	2½"	3"	3½"	4"

The angle of the bends of regular offset shall not be more than 76 degrees.
The angle of bends of eighth bend offsets shall be 45 degrees.

Traps

The radii of all traps shall be as follows:

Diameter	2"	3"	4"	5"	6"
Radius	2"	2½"	3"	3½"	4"

The caulking room at spigot end shall not be less than 5".
The seal to be not less than 2½".

Combination Y and Eighth Bends and Upright Y's

These are produced by combining a regular full Y with a regular eighth bend less the hub of the branch of the former and less the spigot end of the latter.

SOIL PIPE AND PIPE JOINTS

Before taking up "roughing-in" work, the plumbing student should know something about soil pipe and the large variety of fittings used; he should have a thorough knowledge of the joints, how they are made up, and the reason for using certain fittings, etc. There are two kinds of soil pipe used for drainage work, classified according to the kind of joint and material, as

1. Bell and spigot cast iron pipe
    a. Plain
    b. Coated
    c. Lined
    d. Standard weight
    e. Extra heavy

2. Wrought Pipe, Threaded
   (Cast or malleable iron recessed threaded fittings; Durham system)
   The thickness of cast iron pipe for any given size varies according to class as 1 standard, 2 medium, 3 extra heavy.
   The weight known as standard is sometimes used on buildings under four stories in height, and for vent pipe and soil pipe extensions above the highest fixture.
   Extra heavy pipe and fittings are used in tall buildings and in most ordinary work for all soil and waste purposes below the highest fixture. The standard length of cast soil pipe for all sizes is five feet, exclusive of bell.

Bell and spigot iron pipe is generally conceded as the best pipe for drainage work; the other kind should never be used, because wrought pipe has a much shorter life than cast iron pipe and the joint, although recessed, tends to collect paper and other foreign matter more so than does the bell and spigot joint because of the burrs left on the ends of wrought pipe when cut and not reamed out.

Another objection is that in installing the pipe, it must be in perfect alignment, otherwise the pipe cannot be screwed into the fitting or vice versa; whereas the bell and spigot joint presents no such difficulty and the work accordingly does not have to be performed with the same degree of precision

Bell and Spigot Joints

A line of pipe is composed of numerous lengths of pipes or units which must be connected by some form of joint so that the junctions will be water and air tight. In the case of cast iron soil pipe, the bell and spigot form of joint is used.

In this joint, each piece is made with an enlarged *hub* or *bell* at one end into which the plain or spigot end of another piece is inserted when laying. The joint is then made tight by cement, oakum, lead, rubber or other suitable substance which is driven in or caulked into the bell and around the spigot. When a similar joint is made in wrought pipe by means of a cast bell (or hub), it is at times called hub and spigot (poor usage).

In making up the joint, two materials are required:
1. Oakum
2. Lead

Oakum is shredded rope or hemp fibre and should be of the best quality. It usually comes in 50-lb. bales. Some plumbers think that old scrap lead will answer, but this is a mistake because soft lead should be used for reasons later given.

Making up the joint consists of three operations:
1. Packing the oakum
2. Pouring the molten lead
3. Caulking the lead

Packing the Oakum

The plumber first caulks twisted or spun oakum into the annular packing space or socket, similarly to packing a stuffing box on an engine, working it around and then driving it in tightly with a yarning iron and hammer.

The socket should be packed at least half full of the oakum. A good quantity of oakum packed tightly and a less quantity of lead makes the best job.

The oakum must be thoroughly compressed so as to make a solid bed for the lead. Oakum, even without lead, can often be made to hold a heavy pressure of water.

For joints near the ceiling, it is necessary to use a ceiling drop tool to pack the socket. The handle of this tool is quite heavy, so that the yarn may be first forced into the socket by a series of jerking blows with the hand. The offset at the handle provides a surface for blows with a hammer in packing the yarn tightly in the socket.

Pouring the Molten Lead

When the yarn has been tightly compressed in the joint, evenly all around, the next operation is pouring the lead.

It is important that the socket be filled at one pouring, hence first melt up plenty of lead and then dip out of the pot with the pouring ladle an ample supply to fill the socket without a second dipping.

Before pouring, care should be taken to see that there are no projecting strands of oakum, otherwise when the lead is poured these strands will be consumed, leaving minute ducts through the lead to cause leakage.

Care should be taken that socket is quite dry before pouring, as the molten lead would turn any water into steam, causing an explosion.

There should not be any moisture in the joint when the lead is poured, because the sudden generation of steam by contact of the molten lead with the moisture will hurl the lead out of the joint with explosive force, possibly injuring the plumber.

To guard against injury from explosion, the plumber should stand as far away from the ladle as possible and out of range of the direction in which the lead would blow.

If it be necessary to pour a wet joint, first tightly pack the oakum, then sprinkle in a teaspoonful of powdered rosin, or oil if rosin is not available. The object of this is to prevent the flying of the molten lead when it strikes the moisture. Extreme caution, however, should be taken in pouring where there is moisture.

When lead is to be poured into a horizontal joint, a *joint runner* is used.

Never monkey with molten lead; it is no man's friend when it suddenly comes in contact with water.

Sometimes it is necessary to pour a joint upside down. This may be done by placing the joint runner around the pipe and clamping.

Caulking the Lead

After pouring the lead, the next operation is caulking, which is done with a caulking tool. These are similar to yearning tools except that the blade is shorter and heavier. Some caulk while the joint is hot, others after it has cooled. The best method is to caulk moderately tight while the joint is hot so that the lead will better adjust itself to irregularities of the socket walls. After the joint has cooled, the caulking is finished by driving the lead into contact with the spigot surface on one edge and against the inner surface of the bell on the other. Where the joint is fully accessible, regular pattern tools are used.

Similarly, as in yarning operations, there is a multiplicity of special caulking tools to facilitate caulking in close places.

Cutting Soil Pipe

In any job of pipe fitting there will be numerous places where it is necessary to cut a length of pipe to make up the line. This is because the pipe is cast in standard lengths, usually 5 feet, hence unless the distance between the first and last joints of a line be a multiple of 5, there will be an odd length less than 5 feet, necessitating the cutting of a 5 foot length to obtain the short piece of pipe needed to complete the line.

The full 5 foot length will have a bell (or hub) on one end and a spigot (or bead) on the other, called *single bell* pipe.

Evidently, if a length of single bell pipe be cut to obtain a short length, the spigot end would be of no use, resulting in waste. To avoid this, a *double bell* pattern pipe is used; when this is cut, each piece will have a bell so that it may be used. Accordingly, in ordering pipe for any installation, a few lengths of double bell pattern pipe should be included to avoid waste in cutting.

On cutting, first make a chalk mark entirely around the pipe where it is to be cut. This mark should be true, not rambling. A hammer and sharp pointed cold chisel is better for cutting than wheel pipe cutters.

The pipe should be firmly supported on the floor with a block at the cutting line, or preferably on a mound of earth. In cutting, the use of chisel and hammer is safer than cutting with wheel cutters on account of the liability to crack the pipe.

The pipe is easily cracked with wheel cutters because it is often not of uniform thickness throughout and because with the cutters this variation in thickness cannot be so easily detected as with the chisel and hammer.

With the latter, the ear is of great assistance in determining where the pipe is thick or thin as indicated by the sound produced in hammering.

When using a chisel and hammer, the chisel should be narrow and sharply pointed, and the hammer of medium weight.

A difficulty encountered in making up a joint with a cut piece of double bell pipe is that there is no spigot or bead on the end to center the pipe, and care must be taken to keep the cut end centered with the bell so that the packing will be of uniform thickness all around. If in packing the cut end be pushed to one side, it will be difficult to make a tight joint.

Wrought Pipe

Formerly, wrought iron was almost exclusively used in the manufacture of wrought pipe, but because of its expense and also on account of the improved methods in the manufacture of steel pipe, conditions have been reversed and now almost all wrought pipe is made of steel.

The term *wrought iron* is often erroneously used to refer to pipes made to Briggs standard sizes rather than of the material. Hence, in ordering pipe, if iron pipe is wanted instead of steel, care should be taken to specify *genuine wrought iron* or *guaranteed wrought iron* pipe.

It is customary for manufacturers to stamp each length of such pipe as *genuine wrought iron* to distinguish it from steel and *no wrought iron pipe should be accepted* as such without the stamp.

To adapt wrought iron to different pressures, it is regularly made up in several weights as follows:

1. Merchant
2. Standard
3. Extra strong (or heavy)
4. Double extra strong (or heavy)

Merchant pipe is *short weight* pipe. It is necessary to guard against this short weight pipe which formerly was extensively made to meet the demand of sharp jobbers, but now reputable companies have given up the manufacture of such pipe.

Merchant pipe is usually 5 to 10 percent thinner than full weight pipe. It should be carefully avoided in work of any importance, as the extra cost of maintenance will soon overbalance the small difference in first cost. As a precaution against merchant pipe, orders should specify full weight pipe.

For drainage work, no lighter pipe than standard weight should be used. The use of this pipe with recessed threaded fittings constitutes what is known as the Durham System.

This differs from ordinary wrought piping. The object of recessing the fittings is to bring the walls of the pipe and fittings flush with each other to avoid the projecting shoulder, which would form a place for the accumulation of lint and other foreign matter. The recessed fitting does not entirely overcome this trouble because instead of a shoulder there is a pocket due to the recess, and here matter is liable to collect. Aside from this defect, the wrought pipe used in the Durham System is less durable than cast iron. Its principal use is in high buildings because it is lighter than cast iron and takes up less space. Owing to its light weight, it is placed in high buildings with not much more provision being made for supporting its great weight than is made with cast iron in a private dwelling.

Coated Cast Iron Pipe

Standard pipe is dipped in hot asphaltum by the manufacturer to prevent the deteriorating effects of corrosion and to fill up any sand holes, flaws or other defects that may have occurred in manufacture. Extra heavy pipe is also coated in this manner to prevent corrosion; however, it is often left plain so that any defects may be discovered and remedied.

Pipe for Corrosive Wastes

The rapid growth of the use of acids and other corrosives in industrial work, as well as the increasing number of schools, colleges, and hospitals containing chemical laboratories, make more necessary a knowledge of this special plumbing equipment.

Among industrial users, the most common are battery service stations, photo-engravers, manufacturing jewelers, and those industries which manufacture enameled or plated articles and, therefore, must use acids for cleaning the material.

Several kinds of pipes are used to meet the severe requirements of drainage systems for corrosive wastes, such as

1. Non-corrosive metal
2. Lead lined

Non-Corrosive Pipe

This pipe may be cut with a cold chisel and hammer, just like cast iron soil pipe, but the metal is so hard that the chisel will make only a slight scratch on the pipe. Running around the pipe two or three times with the chisel, using about the same weight hammer blows as with cast iron, will cause the pipe to break clean.

A pipe cutter having a coil spring above the specially hardened cutter wheel will save much time on a job.

In making joints on Duriron pipe, asbestos rope, at least 85% pure, should be used in place of hemp or oakum in order to make an acid-proof joint, and the lead should be poured at as low temperature as possible. If too hot, the bell or hub may be cracked while caulking.

Lead-Lined Cast Iron Pipe

This pipe is sometimes used in places where acids enter the drainage system. In making up a joint with lead-lined pipe, the pipe itself should be cut off at a point that will allow for heating the lead over the end of the pipe. When placed in the bell, the hot lead will make a perfect joint, and the iron will be protected from contact with the acids.

Lead-lined pipe may be secured in two forms, screwed and flanged. The former is cut and installed just like steel pipe.

GAS PIPE FITTING

Size of Pipe

In the installation of gas piping, no pipe should be smaller than $3/8$ in. on concealed work and no pipe smaller than ½ in. should be used for concealed horizontal lines. The size of pipe will depend on

1. Length
2. Number of outlets

The method of arriving at the size of pipe needed for various requirements will now be given.

The size of pipe necessary to install considering all conditions depends on:

1. Length of pipe
2. Maximum gas consumption
3. Allowable pressure drop
4. Specific gravity of the gas

Installation of Piping

Standard weight wrought pipe is used with Briggs standard threads. The following table gives the approximate number of threads and length of threaded portions to be cut for each size pipe.

AMOUNT OF THREADING FOR PIPES

Size of Pipe, Inches	Approximate Length of Threaded Portion In Inches	Approximate Number of Threads to Be Cut
3/8	9/16	10
½	¾	10
¾	¾	10
1	7/8	10
1¼	1	11
1½	1	11
2	1	11
2½	1½	12
3	1½	12
4	1¾	13

The pipe should first be cut off square and proper care taken to cut perfect thread. In making up the joints, the threads of both male and female ends must be perfectly clean.

The bristles of the brush should be stiff. Too much care cannot be given to this part of the work as a perfect joint cannot be made with dirty threads.

An approved jointing compound should be used, and it should be put on the male thread sparingly yet the entire threaded portion should be covered. Sealing wax or any material or compound known as "gas fitters cement" should not be used in making up the joints. All branches should be taken from the top or side of a horizontal and not from the bottom. When ceiling outlets are taken from horizontal pipe, the branch should be taken from the side of the piping and carried in a horizontal direction, preferably not less than 6 inches. In bending pipe, care should be taken that it does not kink, and not bent to radii less than in the following table.

MINIMUM RADII FOR BENDS

Size of Pipe (Inches)	3/8	1/2	3/4	1	1¼	1½	2
Minimum Radius of Bends (Inches)	3	4	6	8	12	15	18

In the installation of pipe, care should be taken that it is properly supported and not subjected to any unnecessary strain.

The following table gives the maximum spacing of supports for various size pipes.

Spacing of Supports

3/8 in. or 1/2 in. pipe .... 6 ft.
3/4 in. or 1 in. pipe .... 8 ft.
1¼ in. or larger (horizontal) .... 10 ft.
1¼ in. or larger (vertical) .... Every floor level

When the length of pipe is shorter than that given in the above table, it should be adequately supported. Wherever there is a change of direction of 45° or more, or a branched fitting is used, support should be provided on at least one side of the bend or fitting, preferably within 6 in. of this joint, unless other supports render this unnecessary.

Pipe straps or iron hooks should not be used for fastening pipe of a size over 2 inches. Beyond this size, when the pipe is horizontal and is to be fastened to the floor joists or beams, pipe hangers should be used; when the pipe is horizontal and is to be fastened to the wall, hook plates should be used.

When pipes run crosswise to beams, do not cut the beam to a depth of more than one-fifth of the depth of the timber. This cutting should be as near the support of the beam as possible and in no case should it be further from a support than one-sixth of the span.

When possible, run pipes parallel with the beams to avoid cutting and resulting weakening of the beams. Horizontal lines should have some pitch to provide for drainage of any condensed liquid, especially where pipes are exposed to cold. At the lowest point on a trapped section where such cannot be avoided, a T with a proper length nipple (looking down) and a cap should be provided to facilitate the removal of the liquid.

The size drip to use should be in proportion to the amount of exposed section which drains into it.

Where an offset is necessary, as in the case of an increase in the thickness of a wall, the offset should be made with 45° elbows in preference to 90° elbows to reduce friction to flow and reduce the likelihood of stoppage. Where piping is run in a cellar, it should be hung from the ceiling or joists, and not supported on the walls.

Prohibited Fittings

In reducing the size of pipes, a bushing should not be used; the connection should be made with a reducer. Unions should not be used, as they are liable to leak if not made up properly. Use instead a right and left coupling. On concealed piping, swing joints made by use of combination of fittings should not be used.

DRAINAGE FITTINGS

The system of pipe fittings commonly known as *drainage fittings* consists of screwed fittings having *recessed threads*. These differ from ordinary screwed fittings and the distinction should be carefully noted. Drainage fittings are sometimes called Durham fittings after the name of the inventor.

The object of the recessed threads is to bring the surface of the pipe and surface of the fitting flush with each other so that there not be any projecting shoulder to catch solid matter

Theoretically, there should be no recess or pocket in which matter could lodge, that is the inside surface of fitting and pipe at the joint should be continuous, the end of the pipe being in contact with the shoulder of the fitting.

In practice, it would require very fine adjustment of the pipe dies to bring the end of the pipe in contact with the shoulder when the pipe was screwed into the fitting with the proper tightness, and would not be advisable as it would be necessary to change the adjustment for each fitting to allow for any variation in the cut and condition of the surface.

The proper method is to adjust the die so that when the joint is made up, the end of the pipe will be very close but not in contact with the shoulder.

On vent lines, either drainage or ordinary fittings may be used.

Since drainage fittings are used with wrought pipe, the installation is lighter than cast iron pipe and soil fittings. This adapts the system, especially to high buildings, as the weight to be supported is less. Moreover, less space is required which, for small installations, makes it possible to conceal stacks in the frame of the building.

One disadvantage of the Durham system is that the wrought pipe is not as durable as cast iron or soil pipe. This can be offset by using extra heavy pipe; however, in this connection it should be noted that the extra thickness of the pipe is had at the expense of reducing the inside diameter of the pipe.

Drainage fittings are made either in cast iron or malleable iron, the latter made from the cast iron patterns. They are coated with heated asphaltum excepting those for use in New York city which are not coated. They are chamfered to prevent damage to the threads and permit easy entrance of the pipe in making up joints.

Fittings, such as TY's, crosses intended to connect with waste or soil lines from baths, closets, etc., have inlets tapped, pitched ¼-inch to the foot so that these lines will have proper pitch to drain.

The inlets on reducing fittings are always the smallest openings.

Drainage Fittings for Wall Closets

Special fittings may be obtained for use wherever back or wall outlet closets are installed in batteries. They are especially adaptable for buildings of reinforced concrete construction. Using these fittings in connection with wall hung closets eliminates the necessity of cutting and thus weakening the floors, as the horizontal waste line is entirely above the floor.

Before the advent of these fittings, it was always necessary to suspend the horizontal waste line of a battery of closets from the ceiling below, unless a groove was made in the floor, or the floor of the toilet room raised. All of these methods are objectionable but are necessary where ordinary drainage fittings are used. These fittings are tapped for the closet connection at different distances from the center of the run, so that when the closets in a battery are set in line and the fittings placed in consecutive order according to the tapping numbers given them, the waste line is given a pitch.

Each fitting takes the place of a drainage tee, nipple, and Y (required where regular fittings are used) reducing the number of joints for each closet and simplifying the piping.

When six or less closets are installed in a single battery, it is recommended that fittings with the odd tapping numbers be specified, which will give the maximum amount of pitch. As an example, when fittings for six closets are required, the first fitting from the stack should be specified with "Tapping No. 1"; second, "Tapping No. 3"; third, "Tapping No. 5," etc. with "Tapping No. 11" for the sixth closet. The differences in the tapping dimensions will give additional pitch to the horizontal drainage waste line. For sanitary reasons, the long turn fittings should be used wherever right or left hand and single or double.

Combined Soil and Packed Drainage Fittings

This type of fitting is used extensively in California and other Western sections. Such fittings are designed to connect fixtures to soil pipes without the use of lead pipe and wiped joints.

SCREWED PIPE FITTINGS

Since pipe cannot be obtained in unlimited lengths, and the fact that in practically all pipe installations there are numerous changes in directions, branches, etc., pipe fittings have been devised for the necessary connections. By definition, the term *pipe fittings* is used to denote all those fittings that may be attached to pipes in order (1) to alter the direction of a pipe, (2) to connect a branch with a main, (3) to close an end, and (4) to connect two pipes of different sizes.

There is undue multiplicity of fittings on the market and the supply house that keeps all of them is indeed hard to find, hence in *pipe fitting* it is advisable to use only the simplest fittings, because special or unusual forms are hard to get and costly.

All these various fittings may be classed:

1. With respect to material, as
    a. Cast iron
    b. Malleable iron
    c. Brass
    d. Steel: cast and forged

2. With respect to design, as
    a. Plain
    B. Beaded
    C. Band

3. With respect to the method of connecting, as
    a. Screwed
    B. Flanged
    C. Ball and spigot

4. With respect to strength, as
    a. Standard
    b. Extra strong (or heavy)
    c. Double extra strong (or extra heavy)

5. With respect to the surface, as
    a. Black
    b. Galvanized

6. With respect to finish, as
    a. Rough
    b. Semi-finished
    c. Polished

7. With respect to service, as
   a. Gas
   b. Steam
   c. Hydraulic (heavy pressure)
   d. Drainage
   e. Railing
   f. Sprinkler

8. With respect to thread, as
   a. Briggs' Standard
   b. Recessed threaded
   c. Fine thread

The following definitions relating to pipes, joints, and fittings will be found helpful to the pipe fitter, and those desiring to acquire a knowledge of the subject.

DEFINITIONS

Armstrong Joint: A two-bolt, flanged or lugged connection for high pressures. The ends of the pipes are peculiarly formed to properly hold a gutta-percha ring. It was originally made for cast iron pipe. The two bolt feature has much to commend it. There are various substitutes for this joint, many of which employ rubber in place of gutta-percha; others use more bolts in order to reduce the cost.

Bell and Spigot Joint:
1. The usual term for the joint in cast iron pipe. Each piece is made with an enlarged diameter or bell at one end into which the plain or spigot end of another piece is inserted when laying. The joint is then made tight by cement, oakum, lead, rubber, or other suitable substance, which is driven in or caulked into the bell and around the spigot. When a similar joint is made in wrought pipe by means of a cast bell (or hub), it is at times called hub and spigot joint (poor usage). Matheson joint is a name applied to a similar joint in wrought pipe which has the bell formed from the pipe.
2. Applied to fittings or valves, means that one end of the run is a "bell" and the other end is a "spigot," similar to those used on regular cast iron pipe.

Bonnet:
1. A cover used to guide and enclose the tail end of a valve spindle.
2. A cap over the end of a pipe

Branch: The outlet or inlet of a fitting not in line with the run but which may make any angle.

Branch Ell:
1. Used to designate an elbow having a back outlet in line with one of the outlets of the "run." It is also called a heel outlet elbow.
2. Incorrectly used to designate side outlet or back outlet elbow.

Branch Pipe: A very general term, used to signify a pipe either cast or wrought, that is equipped with one or more branches. Such pipes are used so frequently that they have acquired common names such as tees, crosses, side or back outlet elbows, manifolds, double branch elbows, etc. The term branch pipe is generally restricted to such as do not conform to usual dimensions.

Branch Tee (header): A tee having many side branches. (See Manifold)

Bull Head Tee: A tee, the branch of which is larger than the run.

Bushing: A pipe fitting for the purpose of connecting a pipe with a fitting of larger size, being a hollow plug with internal and external threads to suit the different diameters.

Card Weight Pipe: A term used to designate standard or full weight pipe, which is the Briggs' standard thickness of pipe.

Close Nipple: One of the length of which is about twice the length of a standard pipe thread and is without any shoulder.

Coupling: A threaded sleeve used to connect two pipes. Commercial couplings are threaded to suit the exterior thread of the pipe. The term coupling is occasionally used to mean any jointing device and may be applied to either straight or reducing sizes.

Cross: A pipe fitting with four branches arranged in pairs, each pair on one axis, and the axis at right angles. When the outlets are otherwise arranged, the fittings are branch pipes or specials.

Cross Over: A fitting with a double offset, or shaped like the letter U with the ends turned out. It is only made in small sizes and used to pass the flow of one pipe past another when the pipes are in the same plane.

Cross Over Tee: A fitting made along the lines similar to cross over, but having at one end two openings in a tee head the plane of which is at right angles to the plane of the cross over bend.

Cross Valve:
1. A valve fitted on a transverse pipe so as to open communication at will between two parallel lines of piping. Much used in connection with oil and water arrangements, especially on shipboard.
2. Usually considered as an angle vale with a back outlet in the same plane as the other two openings.

Crotch: A fitting that has a general shape of the letter Y. Caution should be exercised not to confuse the crotch and wye ("Y").

Double Branch Elbow: A fitting that, in a manner, looks like a tee, or as if two elbows had been shaved and then placed together, forming a shape something like the letter Y or a crotch.

Double Sweep Tee: A tee made with easy curves between body and branch, that is, the center of the curve between run and branch lies outside the body.

Drop Elbow: A small sized ell that is frequently used where gas is put into a building. These fittings have wings cast on each side. The wings have small countersunk holes so that they may be fastened by wood screws to a ceiling or wall or framing timbers.

Drop Tee: One having the same peculiar wings as the drop elbow.

Dry Joint: One made without gasket or packing or smear of any kind, as a ground joint.

Elbow (Ell): A fitting that makes an angle between adjacent pipes. The angle is always 90 degrees, unless another angle is stated. (See Branch, Service and Union Ell.)

Extra Heavy: When applied to pipe, means pipe thicker than standard pipe; when applied to valves and fittings, indicates goods suitable for a working pressure of 250 pounds per square inch.

Header: A large pipe into which one set of boilers is connected by suitable nozzles or tees, or similar large pipes from which a number of smaller ones lead to consuming points. Headers are often used for other purposes – for heaters or in refrigeration work. Headers are essentially branch pipes with many outlets, which are usually parallel. Largely used for tubes or water tube boilers.

Hydrostatic Joint: Used in large water mains, in which sheet lead is forced tightly into the bell of a pipe by means of the hydrostatic pressure of a liquid.

Lead Joint:
1. Generally used to signify the connection between pipes which is made by pouring molten lead into the annular space between a bell and spigot, and then making the lead tight by caulking.
2. Rarely used to mean the joint made by pressing the lead between adjacent pieces, as when a lead gasket is used between flanges.

Lead Wool: A material used in place of molten lead for making pipe joints. It is lead fiber, about as coarse as fine excelsior, and when made in a strand, it can be caulked into the joints, making them very solid.

Line Pipe: Special brand of pipe that employs recessed and taper thread couplings, and usually greater length of thread than Brigg's standard. The pipe is also subjected to higher test.

Lip Union:
1. A special form of union characterized by the lip that prevents the gasket being squeezed into the pipe so as to obstruct the flow.
2. A ring union, unless flange is specified.

Manifold:
1. A fitting with numerous branches used to convey fluids between a large pipe and several smaller pipes. (See Branchy Tee.)
2. A header for a coil.

Matheson Joint: A wrought pipe joint made by enlarging one end of the pipe to form a suitable lead recess, similar to the bell of a cast iron pipe, and which receives the male or spigot end of the next length. Practically the same style of joint as used for cast iron pipe.

Medium Pressure: When applied to valves and fittings, means suitable for a working pressure of from 125 to 175 pounds per square inch.

Needle Valve: A valve provided with a long tapering point in place of the ordinary valve disc. The tapering point permits fine graduation of the opening. At times called a needle point valve.

Nipple: A tubular pipe fitting usually threaded on both ends and under 12 inches in length. Pipe over 12 inches is regarded as cut pipe. (See Close, Short, Shoulder and Space Nipples.)

Reducer:
1. A fitting having a larger size at one end than at the other. Some have tried to establish the term "increaser" – thinking of direction of flow – but this has been due to misunderstanding of the trade custom of always giving the largest size of run of a fitting first; hence, all fittings having more than one size are reducers. They are always threaded inside unless specified flanged or for some special joint.
2. Threaded type, made with abrupt reduction.
3. Flanged pattern with taper body.
4. Flanged eccentric pattern with taper body, but flanges at 90 degrees to one side of body.
5. Misapplied at times to a reducing coupling.

Run:
1. A length of pipe that is made of more than one piece of pipe.
2. The portion of any fitting having its end "in line" or nearly so, in contradistinction to the branch or side opening, as of a tee. The two main openings of an ell also indicate its run; and where there is a third opening on an ell, the fitting is a "side outlet" or "back outlet" elbow, except that when all three openings are in one plane and the back outlet is in line with one of the run openings, the fitting is a "heel outlet elbow" or a "single sweep tee" or sometimes a "branch tee."

Rust Joint: Employed to secure rigid connection. The joint is made by packing the intervening space tightly with a stiff paste which oxidizes the iron, the whole rusting together and hardening into a solid mass. It generally cannot be separated except by destroying some of the pieces. One recipe is 80 pounds cast iron borings or filings, 1 pound sal-ammoniac, 2 pounds flowers of Sulphur, mixed to a paste with water.

Service Ell: An elbow having an outside thread on one end. Also known as a *street ell*.

Service Pipe: A pipe connecting mains with a dwelling.

Service Tee: A tee having inside thread on one end and on branch, but outside thread on the other end of run. Also known as *street tee*.

Short Nipple: One whose length is a little greater than that of two threaded lengths or somewhat longer than a close nipple. It always has some unthreaded portion between the two threads.

Shoulder Nipple: A nipple any length, which has a portion of pipe between two pipe threads. As generally used, however, it is a nipple about halfway between the length of a close nipple and a short nipple.

Space Nipple: A nipple with a portion of pipe or shoulder between the two threads. It may be of any length long enough to allow a shoulder.

Standard Pressure: A term applied to valves and fittings suitable for a working steam pressure of 125 pounds per square inch.

Street Elbow: An elbow having an outside thread on one end; also called *service ell*.

Tee: A fitting, either cast or wrought, that has one side outlet at right angles to the run. A single outlet branch pipe. (See Branch, Bull Head, Cross Over, Double Sweep, Drop, Service, and Union Tees.)

Union: The usual trade term for a device used to connect pipes. It commonly consists of three pieces which are first, the thread end fitted with exterior and interior threads; second, the bottom end fitted with interior threads and a smaller exterior shoulder; and third, the ring which has made an inside flange at one end while the other end has an inside thread like that on the exterior of the thread end. A gasket is placed between the thread and bottom ends, which are drawn together by the ring. Unions are very extensively used, because they permit of connections with little disturbance of the pipe positions.

Union Ell: An ell with a male or female union at one end.

Union Fitting: An elbow or tee combined with a union.

Union Joint: The pipe coupling, usually threaded, which permits disconnection without disturbing other sections.

Union Tee: A tee with male or female union at connection on one end of run.

Wiped Joint: A lead joint in which the molten solder is poured upon the desired place, after scraping and fitting the parts together, and the joint is wiped up by hand with a moleskin or cloth pad while the metal is in a plastic condition.

Wye(y): A fitting either cast or wrought that has one side outlet at any angle other than 90 degrees. The angle is usually 45 degrees, unless another angle is specified. The fitting indicated by the letter Y.

Cast Iron Fittings

Standard beaded or flat band fittings of cast iron are suitable for 125 lbs. steam or 175 lbs. water pressure. These fittings will require from 1,000 to 2,500 lbs. to burst them, the large factor of safety is necessary in their use because of the strain due to expansion, contraction, weight of piping, settling and water hammer, and quality of the work of erecting, together with the possibility that they will not run uniform. For steam pressures above 125 lbs., extra heavy fittings should be used.

Malleable Iron Fittings

Standard beaded or flat band fittings of malleable iron are intended for steam pressures up to 150 pounds. Such fittings have at various times been subjected to hydraulic pressures of from 2,000 to 4,000 lbs. without bursting them. It would accordingly seem that they would be safe for 250 lbs. steam pressure.

If proper care be exercised in fitting and using them, they will undoubtedly be found satisfactory for pressures up to 500 lbs., but as all fittings are subject to strain due to expansion, contraction, and making up the joints, they are not recommended for pressures over 150 lbs. In fact, since extra heavy fittings cost only a little more, it is in general not economical to use standard fittings for pressures above 150 lbs.

Standard plain pattern malleable fittings are used for low pressure gas and water, house plumbing, and railing work.

Brass Fittings

These are made in both standard, extra heavy, and cast iron patterns (iron pipe sizes), and are used for brass feed water pipes where bad water makes steel pipes undesirable. The standard brass fittings are usually made in sizes ¼ to 3 inches, suitable for 125 lbs. pressure; extra heavy fittings, $1/8$ to 6 inches, suitable for 150 lbs. pressure; cast iron patterns in all sizes, suitable for 250 lbs.

Semi-Steel Fittings

Extra heavy semi-steel flanged fittings as listed by Kelly & Jones and others can be had in stock sizes from 1½ to 8 inches, tested to 2,000 lbs. hydraulic pressure and are recommended for 800 lbs. pressure. These fittings are regularly finished with male face, unless otherwise ordered.

Cast Steel Fittings

These are made extra heavy with screwed or flanged ends. The screwed fittings are listed in sizes from 3 to 6 inches. The 3 to 4½ inch sizes, inclusive, are tested for 1,500 lbs. hydrostatic pressure, and the 5 and 6 inch sizes for 1,200 lbs. pressure.

The radii of these fittings are larger than the ordinary, thereby reducing friction. They are suitable for the working pressures just given when used in hydraulic installations in which shock is absorbed or so slight as to be negligible.

Ordinarily, these fittings, when subject to shock, should not be used for working pressures higher than 65% of the hydrostatic test pressure, and where shock is severe, 50%, or even 40%, will be more conservative. Installations of this character should always be protected by shock absorbers placed to the best advantage.

Forged Steel Fittings

The extra heavy hydraulic forged steel screwed fittings are suitable for superheated steam up to 2,350 lbs. pressure, a total temperature of 800°F, also for cold water or oil working pressures up to 3,000 lbs. hydrostatic pressure.

They are regularly made from solid forgings in sizes ranging from ½ to 2½ inches, inclusive, and are tested to 3,000 lbs. hydraulic pressure. The double extra heavy pattern is suitable for cold water or oil working pressures up to 6,000 lbs. hydrostatic pressure. They are regularly made from solid forgings in sizes ranging from $^3/_8$ to 2 inches, inclusive, and are tested to 6,000 lbs. hydrostatic pressure.

The Various Fittings

There is a great multiplicity of fittings due to the many modifications of each class of fittings, and the several weights and different metals of which they are made. A list of names of these fittings may be divided into several groups, classified with respect to the use made of the fittings, as

1. Extension or Joining
    a. Nipples
    b. Lock Nuts
    c. Couplings
    d. Offsets
    e. Joints
    f. Unions

2. Reducing or Enlarging
    a. Bushings
    b. Reducers

3. Directional
    a. Offsets
    b. Elbows
    c. Return bends

4. Branching
    a. Side Outlet Elbows
    b. Back Outlet Return Bends
    c. Tees
    d. Y Branches
    e. Crosses

5. Shut Off or Closing
    a. Plugs
    b. Caps
    c. Blind Flanges

6. Union or "Make Up"
   a. Union Elbows
   b. Union Tees

1. **EXTENSION OF JOINING FITTINGS**

   Nipples:

   By definition, a nipple is a *piece of pipe under 12 inches in length threaded on both ends*; pipe over 12 inches long is regarded as cut pipe. With respect to length, nipples may be classed as:
   1. Close
   2. Short
   3. Long

   Where fittings or valves are to be very close to each other, the intervening nipple is just long enough to take the threads at each end, being called a *close nipple*, but if a small amount of pipe intervenes between the threads it is called a *shoulder* or *short nipple*, where a larger amount of bare pipe intervenes it is called a *long nipple*, or *extra long nipple*.

   Extra long nipples are regularly made in sizes ¾ to $1\frac{1}{8}$ x 4; ¾ to 2 x 5; ¾ to 2½ x 6; ¾ to 3½ x 7 and 8; ¾ to 12 x 12, with exception of 11-inch size.

   Nipples having a *right* thread at one end and a *left* thread at the other are generally used in steam heating piping instead of unions.

   Another variety is the *long screw nipple*. This has a long thread on one end on which is a coupling and lock nut, the jamb surface of the coupling and lock nut being faced; the combination forms virtually a union with male and female ends.

   A *tank nipple* has at one end an American Briggs, standard lock nut thread 4 inches long, and at the other a standard pipe thread. A heavy locknut is used on the long thread end.

   Lock Nuts

   These are made with faced end for use on long screw nipples having couplings, and with a recessed or grooved end to hold packing where this is depended upon to make a tight joint.

   The use of lock nipples should be avoided wherever possible, as the joint is not so good as that obtained by a union.

   Couplings

   The ordinary coupling usually comes with the pipie, one coupling to each length of pipe, and is, therefore, classed by some as a part of the pipe rather than a fitting. These are made of wrought or cast metal and of brass; they are regularly threaded right hand, but can be obtained with right and left thread. Right and left couplings have projecting bars or rings to distinguish them from couplings with right thread only. Another form is called an *extension piece*. It differs from the standard coupling in that it has a male thread at one end. There are numerous other types, some being known as *reducers* and others as *joints*.

Joints

There are on the market a number of special couplings or *joints* such as ammonia, Armstrong, bull, bell and spigot, block, bumped, butted, and strapped, Converse, lock, corrugated, crossed artesian, cup, cup and ball, dresser, drive pipe, dry, Eckert, expanded, expansion, Field, flanged, flexible, flush, ground, hydrostatic, inserted, Kimberly, knock off, lead, lead and rubber, line pipe, Matheson, National, Normandy, peeved flanged, Perkins, Petit's Pope, pressure, Riedler, rust, shrink, Siemens, slip, socket, spigot, swing, swivel, thimble, Van Stone, Walker, welded flange, and wiped joint.

Unions

The definition plainly describes the construction of an ordinary union. There are various kinds of unions. The plain union requires a gasket and, incidentally, the two pipes to be joined by the union must be in pretty good alignment to secure a tight joint, because of the flat surfaces which must press against the gasket.

To avoid this difficulty, and also the inconvenience of the gasket, various unions have been devised, having spherical seats and ground joints. The latter, in some, consists of a composition ring bearing against iron, and in others both contact surfaces are composition. Unions are also made entirely of brass with ground joints.

2. REDUCING OR ENLARGING FITTINGS

Bushings

These fittings are often confused with reducers. The function of a bushing is *to connect the male end of a pipe to a fitting of larger size*. It consists of a hollow plug with male and female threads to suit the different diameters.

A bushing may be regarded as either a reducing or an enlarging fitting.

As generally manufactured, bushings 2½ inches and smaller reducing one size are malleable iron; reducing two or more sizes are cast iron, all above 2½ inches are cast iron except brass bushings, which may be obtained in sizes from ¼ to 4 inches.

Bushings are listed by the pipe size of the male thread, thus a "¼ bushing" joins a ¼ fitting to a ⅛ pipe. It is better, however, in ordering, to avoid mistakes to specify both threads, calling for instance the bushing just mentioned a ¼ x ⅛ bushing.

The regular pattern bushing has a hexagon nut at the female end for screwing the bushing into the fitting.

For very close work, the *faced* bushing is used, having in place of the hexagon nut a faced end. This may be used with a long screw pipe and faced lock nut to form a tight joint or to receive a male end fitting for close work.

A form valuable where drainage of the pipe line is desired is the eccentric bushing. Another form is the offset bushing.

Reducers

The term reducer originated from the trade custom of always giving the larger size of a run of a fitting first, and as applied, it means a reducing or enlarging coupling having female threads at both ends, as distinguished from a bushing which has both male and female threads.

3. **DIRECTIONAL FITTINGS**

Offsets

In piping, sometimes part of the pipe line must be in a position parallel to, but not in alignment with the balance of the pipe. An experienced pipe fitter can offset the line by bending the pipe, but ordinarily where the offset or distance between the two pipe axes is of standard dimension, a fitting called an offset can be more conveniently used.

Elbows

Where it is necessary to change the direction of a pipe line in any of several standard and special angles, elbows are used. For gas, water, and steam, the standard angles are 45° and 90° and the special angles are 22½° and 60°.

Cast iron drainage fitting elbows are regularly made with angles of $5^{5}/_{8}°$, 11¼°, 22½°, 45°, 60°, 90°.

Elbow angles measure the degree that the direction is changed. The angle is not the angle between the two arms but the angle between the axis of one arm and the projected axis of the other arm.

Return Bends

These are largely used for making up pipe coils for steam heating and for water tube boilers. They are U-shaped fittings, with a female thread at both ends, and are regularly made in three patterns known as:
 1. Close
 2. Medium
 3. Open

Some manufacturers also make an extra close and extra wide pattern. These patterns represent various widths between the two arms.

There seems to be no standard as to the spacing of the arms for the different patterns, hence for close work the filter should ascertain the center to center dimensions from the manufacturer's catalogue of the make to be used.

For making up so-called "coils" of short lengths of pipe, return bends may be obtained taped with "pitch," that is, tapped so the pipes when screwed into the fitting will not be parallel but spread like the sides of the letter V. Such bends are usually listed with minimum pipe lengths for which the pitch is suitable.

4. **BRANCHING FITTINGS**

Side Outlet Elbows

The two openings of an elbow indicate its *run*; and when there is a third opening, the axis of which is at 90° to the plane of the run, the fitting is a side outlet elbow. These fittings are regularly made in sizes ranging from ¼ to 2 inches, inclusive, with all outlets of equal size, and with side outlet one and two sizes smaller than rim outlets.

In general, it is not well to specify too often fittings of this kind which are not so much in demand as the more usual forms because they are sometimes difficult to get.

Back and Side Outlet Return Bends

These are simply return bends provided with an additional outlet at the back or side. They are regularly made in sizes ranging from ¾ to 3 inches, inclusive, in the close or open patterns, tapped right hand or right and left, as follows:

Side and Back Outlet Return Bends							
Size	¾	1	1¼	1½	2	2½	3
Center to Center, Close	1½	1⁵⁄₈	2¼	2½	3	3⁷⁄₈	4½
Center to Center, Open	2	2³⁄₈	3¹⁄₈	3¼	4	4⁷⁄₈	6¾

Tees

These are the most important and widely used of the branching fittings. Tees, like elbows, are made in a multiplicity of size and pattern. They are used for making a branch at 90° to the main pipe, and always have the branch at right angles.

When the three outlets are of the same size, the fitting is specified by the size of the pipe, as a ½-inch tee; when the branch is of different size than the run outlets, the size of the run is given first as a 1 x ¼ tee; when all three outlets are of different sizes, they are all specified, giving the sizes of the run first as a 1¼ x 1 x 1½ tee.

Y Branches

These are similar to a tee, but have the side outlet at an angle of 45° or 60° instead of 90°. The single 45° Y branches, straight and reducing, are regularly made in sizes ranging from ½ to 4 inches; the double 45° Y branch, in sizes ranging from ½ to 2, inclusive; and the double 60° pattern in the 2 inch and 2 x 1½ inch sizes.

Crosses

A cross is simply an ordinary tee having a back outlet opposite the branch outlet. The axes of the four outlets are in the same plane and at right angles to each other. Crosses, like tees, are made in a multiplicity of sizes.

Regarding it as a tee with a back outlet, the tee part is made in various combinations of sizes, similar to ordinary tees, but the back outlet is always the same size as the opposite outlet, or side outlet, of the tee part.

5. **SHUT OFF OR CLOSING FITTINGS**

Plugs

For closing the end of a pipe or a fitting having a female thread, a plug is used. Plugs are made of cast iron, malleable iron, and brass.

Usually a square head or four side countersunk is used for the small sizes, and a hexagon head for the larger sizes.

Ordinary plugs are made in sizes ranging from $1/8$ to 12 inches inclusive.

Caps

For closing the end of a pipe or fitting having a male thread, a cap is used. These, like plugs, are made of cast iron, malleable iron, and brass. Plain and flat band or beaded caps are regularly made in sizes from $1/8$ to 6 inches, inclusive; cast iron caps from $3/8$ to 15 inches, inclusive, being of plain pattern 2 inches and smaller and of ribbed pattern 2½ inches and larger.

Blind Flanges

These (sometimes called *blank flanges*) are simply cast iron discs for closing flanged fittings or flanged pipe lines.

Flanges are furnished smooth face and not drilled, unless otherwise ordered. An important item in regard to flanges is the drilling.

6. **UNION OR MAKE-UP FITTINGS**

Union Elbow and Union Tees

The frequent use of unions in pipe lines is desirable for convenience in case of repairs. Where the union is combined with a fitting, the advantage of a union is obtained with only one threaded joint instead of two, as in the case of a separate union. A disadvantage of union fittings is that they are not as a rule so easily obtainable as ordinary fittings.

Expansion of Steam Pipes

The linear expansion and contraction of pipe due to differences of temperature of the fluid carried and the surrounding air must be cared for by suitable expansion joints or bends.

GLOSSARY OF PLUMBING TERMS

TABLE OF CONTENTS

	Page
Accepted Standards.....Building Main	1
Building Sewer.....Dry Vent	2
Dual Vent.....Indirect Waste Pipe	3
Interconnection.....Plumbing	4
Plumbing Fixtures.....Sewage Treatment Plant	5
Side Vent.....Water Main	6
Water-Service Pipe.....Yoke Vent	7

GLOSSARY OF PLUMBING TERMS

A

ACCEPTED STANDARDS
Accepted standards are the standards cited in the manual, or other standards approved by the authority having jurisdiction over plumbing.

AIR GAP
The air gap in a water-supply system for plumbing fixture is the vertical distance between the supply-fitting outlet (spout) and the highest possible water level in the receptor when flooded.
If the plane at the end of the spout is at an angle to the surface of the water, the mean gap is the basis for measurement.

APPROVED
Approved means accepted as satisfactory to the authority having jurisdiction over plumbing.

AREA DRAIN
An area drain is a drain installed to collect surface or rain water from an open area.

B

BACKFLOW
Backflow means the flow of water into a water-supply system for any source except its regular one. Back siphonage is one type of backflow.

BACKFLOW CONNECTION
A backflow connection is any arrangement whereby backflow can occur.

BACK VENT
A back vent is a branch vent installed primarily for the purpose of protecting fixture traps from self-siphonage.

BRANCH
A branch is any part of a piping system other than a main. (See Main.)

BRANCH INTERVAL
A branch interval is a length of soil or waste stack corresponding in general to a story height, but in no case less than 8 feet, within which the horizontal branches from one floor or story of the building are connected to the stack.

BRANCH VENT
A branch vent is any vent pipe connecting from a branch of the drainage system to the vent stack.

BUILDING DRAIN
The building (house) drain is that part of the lowest horizontal piping of a building-drainage system which receives the discharge from soil, waste, and other drainage pipes inside the walls of the building and conveys it to the building (house) sewer beginning 5 feet outside the inner face of the building wall.

BUILDING-DRAINAGE SYSTEM
The building-drainage system consists of all piping provided for carrying waste water, sewage, or other drainage from the building to the street sewer or place of disposal.

BUILDING MAIN
The building main is the water-supply pipe including fittings and accessories, from the water (street) main or other source of supply to the first branch of the water-distributing system.

BUILDING SEWER

The building (house) sewer is that part of the horizontal piping of a building-drainage system extending from the building drain 5 feet outside of the inner face of the building wall to the street sewer or other place of disposal (a cesspool, septic tank, or other type of sewage-treatment device or devices) and conveying the drainage of but one building site.

BUILDING SUBDRAIN

A building (house) subdrain is that portion of a drainage system which cannot drain by gravity into the building sewer.

C

CIRCUIT VENT

A circuit vent is a group vent extending from in front of the last fixture connection of a horizontal branch to the vent stack.

COMBINATION FIXTURE

Combination fixture is a trade term designating an integral combination of one sink and one or two laundry trays in one fixture.

CONTINUOUS-WASTE-AND-VENT

A continuous-waste-and-vent is a vent that is a continuation of and in a straight line with the drain to which it connects. A continuous-waste-and-vent is further defined by the angle of the drain and vent at the point of connection make with the horizontal; for example, vertical continuous-waste-and-vent, 45 continuous-waste-and-flat (small angle) continuous-waste-and-vent.

CONTINUOUS WASTE

A waste from two or more fixtures connected to a single trap.

CROSS-CONNECTION

See: INTERCONNECTION

D

DEVELOPED LENGTH

The developed length of a pipe is its length along the center line of the pipe and fittings.

DIAMETER

Unless specifically stated, the term diameter means the nominal diameter as designated commercially.

DISTANCE

The distance or difference in elevation between two sloping pipes is the distance between the intersection of their center lines with the center line of the pipe to which both are connected.

DOUBLE OFFSET

A double offset is two offsets installed in succession or series in the same line.

DRAIN

A drain or drain pipe is any pipe which carries water or waterborne wastes in a building drainage system.

DRAINAGE PIPING

Drainage piping is all or any part of the drain pipes of a plumbing system.

DRY VENT

A dry vent is any vent that does not carry water or water-borne wastes.

DUAL VENT
A dual vent (sometimes called a unit vent) is a group vent connecting at the junction of two fixture branches and serving as a back vent for both branches.

E

EFFECTIVE OPENING
The effective opening is the minimum cross-sectional area between the end of the supply-fitting outlet (spout) and the inlet to the controlling valve or faucet. The basis of measurement is the diameter of a circle of equal cross-sectional area.
If two or more lines supply one outlet, the effective opening is the sum of the effective openings of the individual lines or the area of the combined outlet, whichever is the smaller.

F

FIXTURE BRANCH
A fixture branch is the supply pipe between the fixture and the water-distributing pipe.
FIXTURE DRAIN
A fixture drain is the drain from the trap of a fixture to the junction of the drain with any other drain pipe.
FIXTURE UNIT
A fixture unit is a factor so chosen that the load-producing values of the different plumbing fixtures can be expressed approximately as multiples of that factor.
FLOOD LEVEL
Flood level in reference to a plumbing fixture is the level at which water begins to overflow the top or rim of the fixture.

G

GRADE
The grade of a line of pipe is its slope in reference to a horizontal plane. In plumbing it is usually expressed as the fall in inches per foot length of pipe.
GROUP VENT
A group vent is a branch vent that performs its functions for two or more traps.

H

HORIZONTAL BRANCH
A horizontal branch is a branch drain extending laterally from a soil or waste stack or building drain, with or without vertical sections or branches, which receives the discharge from one or more fixture drains and conducts it to the soil or waste stack or the building (house) drain.

I

INDIRECT WASTE PIPE
An indirect waste pipe is a waste pipe which does not connect directly with the building drainage system, but discharges into it through a properly trapped fixture or receptacle.

INTERCONNECTION

An interconnection, as the term is used is any physical connection or arrangement of pipes between two otherwise separate building water-supply systems whereby water may flow from one system to the other, the direction of flow depending upon the pressure differential between the two systems.

Where such connection occurs between the sources of two such systems and the first branch from either, whether inside or outside the building, the term cross-connection (American Water Works terminology) applies and is generally used.

J

JUMPOVER
See: RETURN OFFSET.

L

LEADER
A leader or downspout is the water conductor from the roof to the storm drain or other means of disposal.

LOOP VENT
A loop vent is the same as a circuit vent except that it loops back and connects with a soil- or waste-stack vent instead of the vent stack.

M

MAIN
The main of any system of continuous piping is the principal artery of the system to which branches may be connected.

MAIN VENT
See: VENT STACK.

N

NONPRESSURE DRAINAGE
Nonpressure drainage refers to a condition in which a static pressure cannot be imposed safely on the building drain. This condition is sometimes referred to as gravity flow and implies that the sloping pipes are not completely filled.

O

OFFSET
An offset in a line of piping is a combination of elbows or bends which brings one section of the pipe out of line with but into a line parallel with another section.

P

PLUMBING
Plumbing is the work or business of installing in buildings the pipes, fixtures, and other apparatus for bringing in the water supply and removing liquid and water-borne wastes. The term is also used to denote the installed fixtures and piping of a building.

PLUMBING FIXTURES

Plumbing fixtures are receptacles which receive and discharge water, liquid, or water-borne wastes into a drainage system with which they are connected.

PLUMBING SYSTEM

The plumbing system of a building includes the water-supply distributing pipes; the fixtures and fixture traps; the soil, waste, and vent pipes; the building (house) drain and building (house) sewer; and the storm-drainage pipes; with their devices, appurtenances, and connections all within or adjacent to the building.

POOL

A pool is a water receptacle used for swimming or as a plunge or other bath, designed to accommodate more than one bather at a time.

PRESSURE DRAINAGE

Pressure drainage, as used in the manual, refers to a condition in which a static pressure may be imposed safely on the entrances of sloping building drains through soil and waste stacks connected thereto.

PRIMARY BRANCH

A primary branch of the building (house) drain is the single sloping drain from the base of a soil or waste stack to its junction with the main building drain or with another branch thereof.

R

RELIEF VENT

A relief vent is a branch from the vent stack, connected to a horizontal branch between the first fixture branch and the soil or waste stack, whose primary function is to provide for circulation of air between the vent stack and the solid or waste stack.

RETURN OFFSET

A return offset or jumpover is a double offset installed so as to return the pipe to its original line.

RISER

A riser is a water-supply pipe which extends vertically one full story or more to convey water to branches or fixtures.

S

SAND INTERCEPTOR (SAND TRAP)

A sand interceptor (sand trap) is a water-tight receptacle designed and constructed to intercept and prevent the passage of sand or other solids into the drainage system to which it is directly or indirectly connected.

SANITARY SEWER

A sanitary sewer is a sewer designed or used only for conveying liquid or water-borne waste from plumbing fixtures.

SECONDARY BRANCH

A secondary branch of the building drain is any branch of the building drain other than a primary branch.

SEWAGE-TREATMENT PLANT

A sewage-treatment plant consists of structures and appurtenances which receive the discharge of a sanitary drainage system, designed to bring about a reduction in the organic and bacterial content of the waste so as to render it less offensive or dangerous, including septic tanks and cesspools.

SIDE VENT
A side vent is a vent connecting to the drain pipe through a 45° wye.

SIZE OF PIPE AND TUBING
The size of pipe and tubing, unless otherwise stated, is the nominal size by which the pipe or tubing is commercially designated. Actual dimensions of the different kinds of pipe and tubing are given in the specifications applying.

SOIL PIPE
A soil pipe is any pipe which conveys the discharge of water closets or fixtures having similar functions, with or without the discharges from other fixtures.

STACK
Stack is a general term for the vertical main of a system of soil, waste, or vent piping.

STACK-VENT
A stack-vent is the extension of a soil or waste stack above the highest horizontal or fixture branch connected to the stack.

STORM DRAIN
A storm drain is a drain used for conveying rain water, subsurface water, condensate, cooling water, or other similar discharges.

STORM SEWER
A storm sewer is a sewer used for conveying rain water, subsurface water, condensate, cooling water, or other similar discharges.

SUBSOIL DRAIN
A subsoil drain is a drain installed for collecting subsurface or seepage water and conveying it to a place of disposal.

T

TRAP
A trap is a fitting or device so designed and constructed as to provide a liquid trap seal which will prevent the passage of air through it.

TRAP SEAL
The trap seal is the vertical distance between the crown weir and the dip of the trap.

V

VENT
A vent is a pipe installed to provide a flow of air to or from a drainage system or to provide a circulation of air within such system to protect trap seals from siphonage and back pressure.

VENT STACK
A vent stack, sometimes called a main vent, is a vertical vent pipe installed primarily for the purpose of providing circulation of air to or from any part of the building-drainage system.

W

WASTE PIPE
A waste pipe is a drain pipe which receives the discharge of any fixture other than water closets or other fixtures receiving human excreta.

WATER MAIN
The water (street) main is a water-supply pipe for public or community use.

WATER-SERVICE PIPE
　　The water-service pipe is that part of a building main installed by or under the jurisdiction of a water department or company.
WATER-SUPPLY SYSTEM
　　The water-supply system of a building consists of the water-service pipe, the water-distributing pipes, and the necessary connecting pipes, fittings, and control valves.
WET VENT
　　A wet vent is a soil or waste pipe that serves also as a vent.

Y

YOKE VENT
　　A yoke vent is a vertical of 45° relief vent of the continuous-waste-and-vent type formed by the extension of an upright wye-branch or 45° wye-branch inlet of the horizontal branch to the stack. It becomes a dual yoke vent when two horizontal branches are thus vented by the same relief vent.

www.ingramcontent.com/pod-product-compliance
Lightning Source LLC
Chambersburg PA
CBHW080324020526
44117CB00035B/2641